PIE
school
❖ Lessons in ❖
FRUIT, FLOUR, and BUTTER

PIE
school

❧ Lessons in ❧
FRUIT, FLOUR, and BUTTER

KATE LEBO

Photography by Rina Jordan

SASQUATCH BOOKS
SEATTLE

Printed in China

Published by Sasquatch Books

20 19 18 17   9 8 7 6 5

Editor: Gary Luke
Project editor: Michelle Hope Anderson
Design: Anna Goldstein
Photographs: Rina Jordan
Food styling: Jean Galton
Prop styling: Jenn Elliott Blake
Copy editor: Diane Sepanski

Library of Congress Cataloging-in-Publication Data is available.

ISBN: 978-1-57061-910-6

Sasquatch Books
1904 Third Avenue, Suite 710
Seattle, WA 98101
(206) 467-4300
www.sasquatchbooks.com
custserv@sasquatchbooks.com

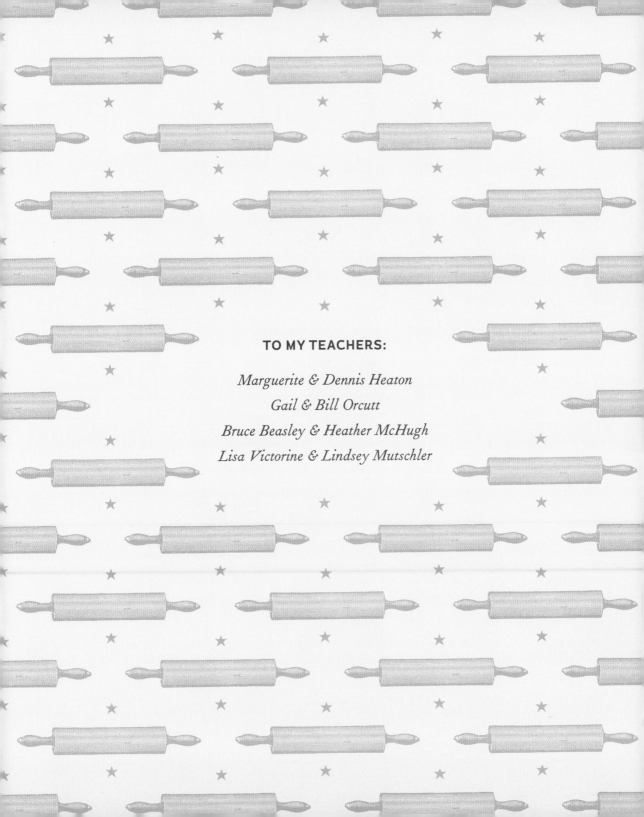

TO MY TEACHERS:

Marguerite & Dennis Heaton
Gail & Bill Orcutt
Bruce Beasley & Heather McHugh
Lisa Victorine & Lindsey Mutschler

contents

introductions

★ ★ ★ ★ ★

Thanks for joining me, fellow pie lover. Let's get acquainted.

I am a writer, teacher, and baker. I founded this school when I was about to graduate from the MFA program at the University of Washington. As a flip answer to the question, "What are you going to do with a creative writing degree?" I said, "Start a pie school," diverting attention from the fact that I wasn't exactly entering a booming job market, and no, I didn't have a plan. With enough repetition, the idea started to seem like a good one. It stuck. I applied for a business license, made a website, and rented a bakery kitchen in Seattle. My students and I tied our aprons and learned together how to make what we could with what we had. They went home with a pie; I went home with plenty to write about. My crazy idea was looking saner by the day.

But the story begins long before that first class.

I was raised in the Pacific Northwest by Iowans. If we're talking in broad generalizations, that means I come from friendly people who'd rather eat than argue.

We lived in a small city just north of Portland, Oregon, that people often mistake for a much larger Canadian city, sometimes so badly they wander to the wrong side of the state and wonder why they don't need their passports to cross the Columbia River. By trading fireflies and snow for volcanoes and rain, my parents gave me a personal topography that is damp, moody, exaggerated, and rich, with the conquered beauty of the Discovery Channel and the lurking wildness of the West.

I learned the geography of my region at the grocery store. Sweet apples from Wenatchee, pie apples from Skagit Valley. Cherries from Hood River, peaches from Yakima. Strawberries from Cornelius, plums from the neighbors', blueberries from my own backyard. And, of course, blackberries. On mountainsides, on roadsides, in the last bit of forest left in the housing development. Poet Mary Oliver calls them "the black honey of summer." I called them lunch.

My first apartment in Seattle had a view of the Space Needle and the busiest chunk of I-5 in Washington State. I joked that except for the air brakes and car horns, it sounded like the ocean (it sounded like exactly what it was: a 24/7 traffic jam). On Thursday nights, with 90.3 KEXP's hard-core honky-tonk show blaring on my radio, my parents on speed dial, and *Joy of Cooking* cracked on the kitchen counter, I taught myself how to bake.

My culinary romance started with a hunger for making things—I couldn't afford to buy DIY supplies, but I did have to eat. Flour and sugar stood in for fabric and glass, peaches and blueberries for thread and yarn. That's the best explanation I have for what happened when, after baking my way through cookies and cakes and bread, I made my first pie: love. Not with eating it—like *Star Trek* and cats, I can't remember a time I wasn't a big fan of pie. I fell in love with the materials, in love with the process. I was at home. A natural. Easy as pie.

Soon, baking became hopelessly intertwined with writing. I baked to procrastinate on a poem; I baked to have something to blog about; I baked because, unlike writing, I knew when the pie was done and I knew if it was good. I didn't get irritated with pie for being anything but what it was. When I gave it to people, they knew exactly how to respond: with delight, appetite, and thanks. Poems are harder. They should be. I needed baking to comfort myself through the hard parts (i.e., almost every part of writing) and fuel the good parts (pie in one hand, pen in the other). As the grocery bills piled up, I formed a habit of baking that helped teach me the habits of writing. Writing helped me understand that pie is a powerful symbol of American culture. More importantly, pie is a powerful gift. I'm writing this book to share that gift with you and to teach you how to tap into that power in your own kitchen.

Now it's your turn. You and I can talk *about* books but we can't talk *through* them. Forgive me as I make a few assumptions.

You're the sort of person who reads books about pie, so I'm guessing you like to bake. You're also the sort of person who will actually read a cookbook (assuming you're reading these words right now) instead of skimming through for a grocery list, so I'm guessing you like to understand *why* you bake as well as what you bake.

Maybe you get shy around pastry. Maybe you want to figure out how to make your own pie recipes. Maybe you're a pie expert and you've come to learn something new, or to reaffirm that your way is better. And it might be better! For you. Teaching pie is a bit like teaching poetry. All I can do is show you the elements of any good pie (or poem) and help you make them with the techniques that have worked best for me.

Many pie-making methods won't be mentioned in these pages. Store-bought crust, for example. We're going to pretend it doesn't exist. You won't find cream pies or chocolate pies either. Why? My gift is for fruit pie, not cream pie. A bevy of cookbooks have already covered the art of the cream pie far more competently than I could, so I'll leave that to them. You also won't find many food processor or even pastry cutter instructions here. Writer and baker Beth Howard says it best: "Your hands are your best tools." Advance apologies to any ruined manicures.

Here's what you *will* find: a lot of recipes that use seasonal produce. That's my specialty and my obsession. You'll encounter ideas for how to make pie-making the sort of thing you do with what you have on hand. You'll attempt to learn, as I did by writing this book, what it is about pie that people love.

I'm a pie-maker.

You're a pie-maker—or you soon will be.

Welcome to Pie School.

Now, let's go wash our hands.

❖ ON RECIPES ❖

(or, How We Know What We Think We Know)

Some recipes promise perfection, some promise ease. Some promise comfort and health. I can promise only that if you make a pie, you are joining a long line of bakers who thought that delivering food in an edible container was the best idea since the advent of the wheat farmer.

Auguste Escoffier (aka the father of modern French cooking) wrote, "No theory, no formula, and no recipe can take the place of experience." I interpret this statement in two ways.

Experience is the best teacher; our axioms tell us that. With experience as my teacher and my senses as my guide, I've learned how to write recipes, then abandon them altogether, giving precedence to the materials of the pie—the fruit, the weather, my mood—in a way that lets them determine the final outcome. This is what I'll attempt to teach you to do too.

Experience is the best muse, especially when it comes to writing about food. That's why fantastic food writing is, like the best pie, often wedded to the "I." That's why M.F.K. Fisher, Calvin Trillin, Anthony Bourdain, Gabrielle Hamilton, and many of our best food writers all compose in the first person and use personal experience to frame their subjects. That's why personal blogs are a popular (and populist) medium for food writing, and why I began this book by introducing myself. Food is a matter of taste. We understand it best when we understand it subjectively.

Subjectivity flouts the ambitions of the perfect recipe, that magic formula that promises consistent results the way McDonald's promises a consistent Quarter Pounder. They're a necessary fiction that helps us get dinner on the table.

But this book isn't about dinner. It's about dessert. Pie, then, is an opportunity to think about recipes and cooking in a different way—a way that privileges imagination over perfection.

You'll need to read these recipes. I mean *really* read them. Many will tell you to adjust seasonings to taste, which literally means *taste the food* as you're preparing it. The filling should be delicious before baking. If it isn't, or—more likely—if it's just so-so, add salt, lemon, spice, or sugar as needed. You'll know the filling is just right when you don't want to stop eating it.

Tasting as you go may seem obvious to some of you, but others may be used to strictly following recipes, scanning the text for quick measurements, or being told exactly how much *x* to put in *y*. A quick scan isn't going to work very well for my recipes, I'll tell you that right now. Fruit changes from season to season, and it's impossible to predict how juicy or flavorful it will be. Pie plates come in all shapes and sizes, so once again I can't tell you exactly how much fruit will fit perfectly, which affects the amount of sugar and spice and thickener you might or might not use. And ovens! Don't get me started on ovens. I'll write more about that later.

The point is your materials and tools are *your materials and tools*—including your hands, which will handle dough in your particular way. I will give you guidelines to help you judge how much fruit, fat, sugar, and spice to use, but "perfect" pie is a product of good judgment and risk-taking, practice and luck. To me, the perfect recipe is one that helps the reader understand the form of the food (in this case, pie) and leaves the rest open to interpretation.

That said, I understand it's intimidating for a novice baker to freestyle a pie when he or she hasn't even made one yet. That's why you'll find two kinds of recipes here: the kind that teach the form by providing clear guidance and instruction for each step of the way, and the kind that leaves the details up to your imagination and whatever you can find in your pantry.

The best way to make pie is to learn how to trust yourself and follow your nose—and the rest of your senses. That's a poet's advice too. Like a slice of pie, my advice should be taken with a grain of salt: I'm teaching you how to make pie *my* way, knowing everyone brings a unique taste and touch to the mixing bowl. As Richard Hugo writes in the opening pages of *The Triggering Town*, his classic text on poetry-making, "Every moment, I am, without wanting or trying to, telling you to write like me. But I hope you learn to write like you. In a sense, I hope I don't teach you how to write but how to teach yourself how to write." For our purposes, replace "write" with "make pie." Remember that Hugo also wrote, "At all times keep your crap detector on." Which is good advice in general.

⹎ ON OVENS ⹑

Your oven isn't going to behave exactly like mine. It may be cooler, hotter, more temperamental, or more steady. It may even be a convection oven. If that's the case, lucky you.

When it comes to cooking times, you may need to make a choice between my instructions and what you see bubbling and browning in front of you. Always choose the pie over me—it will tell you when it's truly done. I've found that if I'm wondering whether or not the pie is done, it's not done. With a little experience, you'll just check the oven and *know*.

⹎ ON CLICHÉS ⹑

Pie is a powerful symbol of desire. By "desire" I mean appetite and sex. It's a messy promise demurely packaged in dough, a hopelessly sexy treat made of ripe fruit—which, botanically speaking, could also be called an ovary. Warrant's 1990 glam-metal anthem "Cherry Pie" and the 1999 teen flick *American Pie* made sex and pie the stuff of recent pop culture, popularizing an innuendo already ripe for the picking. "American Pie" is, of course, also the title of Don McLean's smash hit about "the day the music died." These artifacts tell us that Americans conflate national identity with sex *and* appetite *and* loss of innocence, all the mythic triggers of Eve's apple wrapped in one of the most calorie-dense substances mankind has ever invented. Talk about temptation.

Pie is also a symbol of femininity ("Almost all women at one time feel the urge to bake an old-fashioned pie") and masculinity ("Frequently the spur is the husband with a yen for a wonderful pie his mother used to make"). If you read old cookbooks closely (these quotes are from the 1965 edition of *Farm Journal's Complete Pie Cookbook*), you'll see the gender stereotypes split between eating and making. Women make; men eat.

I hope that most of us are, by now, irritated with these gender roles; there are plenty of men who like to make pie and as many women who like to eat it. Most modern cookbooks avoid gender stereotypes altogether, opting for a heads-down focus on the art of pie-making, without a look around at the cultural land-scape or an errant pronoun to be found. Bless them. But I'm going to say this as clearly as I can: when you make pie, you engage with very old domestic legends that gird our national identity, our gender politics, and our food history. It's bet-ter to admit that than to ignore how "American as," "easy as," "pie in the sky," and "grandma's apron strings" all shrink-wrap gender, Americana, hard work, and hope into easily digestible sound bites.

Our clichés tell us we think something is easy if it is sweet; that women are sweet; that America is the apple pie, the woman who bakes it, and the man who eats it. The democratizing crust over filling, the practical luxury of eating a sweet you can hold in your hand, how homey a slice looks on farm tables, in bygone urban automats—that's American too. Our clichés tell us the opposite of what we know; we know that pie is not easy to make, nor is the making or eating of it bound by gender, nor is pie a strictly American treat, nor is it even usually apple.

As a poet, I've been trained to look at language as a sign of deeper structures, something that constructs meaning and wields power. To me, a cliché is an X on a treasure map. Something valuable lurks beneath the surface. Like the X-vent of a double crust pie, a cliché invites you to open it for further inspection.

George W. Bush once said, "We ought to make the pie higher." He meant opportunity (I think?), but I mean pie. Let's make it higher. Let's lift it out of midcentury kitschy stereotypes and give it a new job.

Make as much pie as you want to. Eat as much as you want to. Whenever you want. Whoever you are.

How's that for easy as, sweet as, American as pie?

⸙ ON THE DEFINITION OF COMFORT FOOD ⸙

(or, What Is Pie?)

Before we go any further, a few definitions.

In England and Australia, pie is generally a savory substance with a top crust. In America it's a sweet treat that requires a bottom crust to bear the name "pie." That is, unless we're talking about Frito pie, where the crust is a bag of chips, or Boston cream pie, which is a cake baked in a pie pan, or pudding pies, those creamy, crustless Jell-O treats most likely to entart an unsuspecting politician or be sucked down the gullet of a pie-eating champion.

Then there's Ambrose Bierce's salty entry in *The Devil's Dictionary*:

> **PIE, n. An advance agent of the reaper whose name is Indigestion.**

Historical record is mum on whether Bierce was a cake fan or an equal-opportunity dessert hater.

Pie's etymology (and its lack of one sure, specific source) tells us that it is a container of mystery and a mysterious container. The story of the word pie might begin in Medieval Latin, related to *pia*, meaning "pastry." Or it might start with *pica*, also Medieval Latin, meaning "magpie." Or with *pie*, a thirteenth-century French word that later became *magpie*, which got its *mag* from Margaret or Marguerite, a woman's name used in slang English to connote feminine qualities. Especially, in this case, chattering idly.

A magpie is, of course, that long-tailed corvid with the raucous voice, "pied" feathers, and habit of hoarding small, bright objects. *Pie* owes a debt to *magpie* probably because of this collection-of-various-ingredients idea (not the chattering part, though the phrase "shut your piehole" seems on the surface like a possible relative).

Pie is also seventeenth-century slang for "a mass of type jumbled together," which is probably related to the idea of "medley" that the other origins of the word point toward, but which I particularly like because it describes this book and any book: a mass of type jumbled together.

❖ ON LOVE ❖

When I say pie alone isn't what moves us, that the "thing" about pie isn't tellable, I mean that food is never just about food. Its offering is deeper than appetite and deeper than words. Maybe pie is a vehicle for love. Maybe it *is* love, made edible by an oven's worth of heat, an hour's worth of time. When we make and eat pie, maybe it is for us as it was for M.F.K. Fisher when she wrote about hunger:

> *It seems to me that our three basic needs, for food and security and love, are so mixed and mingled and entwined that we cannot straightly think of one without the others. So it happens that when I write of hunger, I am really writing about love and the hunger for it, and warmth and the love of it and the hunger for it . . . and then the warmth and richness and fine reality of hunger satisfied . . . and it is all one.*

❖ ON YOU AND YOUR NEW GF BF ❖
(Gluten-Free Best Friend)

Gluten intolerance can be a hard thing. Anyone who has it and anyone who loves someone who has it knows how hard. When I loved and lived with a man who had celiac disease, he'd joke, "Are you trying to kill me?" when he saw me assembling my pie ingredients, eyeing the flour bag and mixing bowls as Clark Kent might eye a kryptonite paperweight. To me, pie was life; to him, poison. I tried to solve this impossible dilemma by creating gluten-free versions of our favorite pies.

Fortunately, the only pie ingredient a gluten-intolerant person needs to fear is flour (and anything it contaminates). Unfortunately, flour is essential to making the fabled flaky crust we prize so much. Rather than try to replicate that flake with a cupboard's worth of alternative flours, I chose to explore different tastes and textures in simpler recipes. A buckwheat crust, for example, is crumbly and toasty, a little too strong tasting for shy flavors but wonderful around outgoing peaches, apples, or rhubarb. An almond flour crust, too, has a sweet-savory flavor that doesn't complement everything, but works well with creamier flavors like pumpkin or mascarpone. We enjoy our dessert even more when we think of these pies as inventions that have their own set of strengths, not as substitutions that can't measure up to the real thing.

Many of the recipes in this book can be adapted for gluten-free pie-lovers. Substitute buckwheat or almond flour for the wheat flour and use tapioca flour instead of wheat flour for thickening. Be careful of cross-contamination and remain patient with the dough. It won't behave like traditional piecrust. We wouldn't want it to.

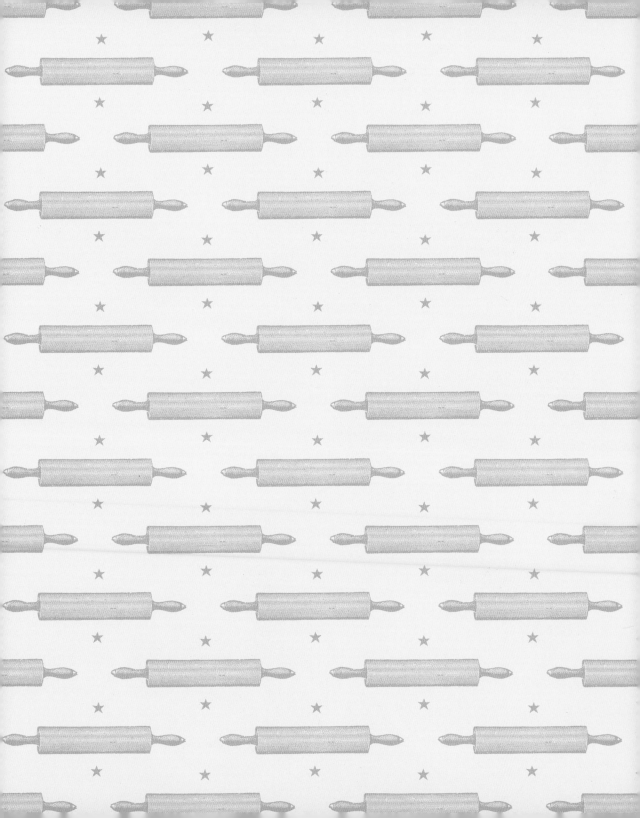

the art and
science of pie

★ ★ ★ ★ ★

*When it comes to cake, if one follows the rules, perfection
is inevitable. But for pastry you must be somewhat of
an interpretive artist as well as a disciplined technician.
You have to develop a sense of the dough.*

—ROSE LEVY BERANBAUM, THE PIE AND PASTRY BIBLE

★ ★ ★ ★ ★

Pie dough has a personality, a certain way it likes to be treated. Pie-crust enforces that treatment by puffing itself up or hunkering down, bringing bakers high and low with its requirements. That's why the cliché "easy as pie" is a joke—for the uninitiated, pie can seem like impossible magic.

Let's say you don't believe in magic. You know fantastic pie is out there waiting to be made, and you'd rather know how it works than wave a wand and pray. You start by reading the experts: Rose Levy Beranbaum's *The Pie and Pastry Bible* and Ken Haedrich's *Pie*, for example. You might turn to the cookbooks of your grandmother's time, since good pie is supposed to be "just like Grandma used to make." Depending on how old Granny is, that could be anything from Betty Crocker and *Joy of Cooking* to *The White House Cook Book*.

Here's what you'll find: confirmation that pie dough requires flour, fat, salt, some sort of liquid, and a light hand. Here's what you won't find: a consistent set of measurements or instructions. There is no magic pie spell. There are thousands of them.

Recipe writing is like a game of telephone. Each cook makes a mark on the source before becoming a source to be marked upon. And if you take into account the currently popular chestnut that "cooking is an art but baking is a science" (implying that cooks can be intuitive, while bakers must follow the rules), the wealth of conflicting pie advice gets even more confusing. Clearly these published recipes—both the super-detailed scientific ones and the taciturn antique ones—helped someone make amazing pie at least once. That's the

$$\star \quad \star \quad \star \quad \star \quad \star$$

conceit of the cookbook, after all. But what are we to do with recipes that don't follow each other's rules?

Start with what these recipes have in common. They want you to use a light touch. To chill the butter and use ice water. To work quickly, confidently, before the heat of your instruments (hands, food processor) melts the butter or their pressure activates too much gluten. Understand how chemical processes craft flake, cook fruit, and thicken juices, and you'll understand why using your senses—in other words, knowing how dough should feel, what it should look like, and how it should smell—is more useful than following any recipe too strictly. You'll develop, as Levy Beranbaum says, "a sense of the dough."

This chapter is devoted to helping you develop that sense.

As you learn, I recommend trying at least several different methods—my favorites have been the tips in *Bubby's Homemade Pies* by Ron Silver and Jen Bervin and the lessons of *Art of the Pie*'s Kate McDermott. These teachers prize following your senses over the mathematic accuracy of *Cook's Illustrated*, which is predicated on the troublesome assumption that a recipe's Platonic ideal exists. Each time you try a new technique, you'll pick up a secret you can use for the next recipe, and you'll be better able to decide what pie-making style works best for you—in terms of fun, convenience, and result.

Pie is a slow food, better handmade in small batches than churned out by machines. If you want to make amazing pie, there's no better time. Start with what you have in front of you right now.

❧ HOW TO MAKE PIECRUST BY HAND ❧

Good pastry is flaky, tender, delicate and evenly
browned. It is not crumbly, but when broken, shows
layers of flat flakes, piled one above the other with
air spaces between. To achieve this result the cook
must be quick and "lighthanded," since pastry
cannot be good if handled roughly or slowly.

—THE VICTORY BINDING OF THE AMERICAN WOMAN'S
COOK BOOK, WARTIME EDITION, 1942

Folk arts are best taught in person. Since I can't be there with you in the kitchen, I've written down as much of the process as I can, as clearly as I can, and included a few illustrations to explain what's too visual to describe. These are narrative instructions for the process of making crust. The next chapter contains five crust recipes that will use this method, and each will include an abbreviated version of these instructions to help you remember the process.

A Word on Flour

All-purpose flour is best. Pastry flour is low in gluten; bread flour is high. Pie requires a Goldilocks-style balance of just the right amount of gluten—enough to give piecrust structure, but not so much that it toughens the crust. I've found that mixing pastry and bread flours still doesn't produce the right blend. Stick to all-purpose and you won't go wrong.

Since we've mentioned bread, let's talk about kneading.

We never knead.

Ever.

That verb is banished from the pie kitchen.

Kneading is a bread verb. It helps develop a strong gluten structure that yeast can make its tiny explosions into, creating a lovely matrix of nooks and crannies that hold jam and butter just so. Pastry is leavened by fat and lightened by evaporating water, neither of which have the puffing power of yeast. A strong gluten structure is a flaky crust's enemy. A too-weak gluten structure makes a delicate, crumbly dough, which has its place in the pie pantheon, but isn't the flaky ideal we're going for. This method is designed to develop just the right amount of gluten and no more than that to create tender, flaky piecrust.

Gluten is the protein that makes wheat nearly irreplaceable in a baker's kitchen. It develops when wheat flour comes into contact with water—itself a neutral process that works to a baker's advantage or disadvantage, depending on what he or she intends to make. If you've heard that piecrust is easy to mess up, this is probably what those whispers were referring to. That means the hardest part of making pie dough starts with water; everything up to water's addition to flour should be stress-free. So, for now, relax!

American-style piecrust privileges the flake above all other textures. That's fine, but let's note that there are other textures, and they can suit the fruit or the occasion just as well. There's crumbly, tender, sturdy, delicate, pale, collapsing, powdery, flavorful, rich, and a whole host of negative descriptors—tough, gluey, hard, chewy, bland. Our goal isn't to always make perfectly flaky dough. Our goal is to achieve the adjectives of our choice on purpose.

A Word on Butter

The higher the quality of the butter, the better it tastes and the easier it is to handle. European butter has a higher fat content, which means less water in the final preparation of the dough (this is a good thing) and a richer flavor (also a good thing). Choose unsalted so you can control the salt content in your dough. If that's not an option, decrease the salt measurement in the dough by ½ teaspoon.

Any kind of fat that stays solid at room temperature can make pastry. That means butter, vegetable shortening, coconut oil, lard, suet, and bear fat are all on the table (assuming you have a license to hunt bear). You'll need about 1 cup chilled fat to 2½ cups flour. You can mess with the types and combinations of fat you use as long as you have about 1 cup of it (I've found that up to 1¼ cups of fat is just fine). Butter is the most flavorful, and with this method it makes a dough that is tender and flaky, in that order. Vegetable shortening is bland, but delivers heavenly flakes and has a higher melting temperature, which means your crust will keep its shape a bit better as it's baked. Lard delivers flavor and flake. Make sure to get leaf lard (see "On Lard," page 63). It's the purest, least porky-tasting fat.

A Word on Water

Ice water binds pieces of flour and fat together while helping the fat stay solid. Too-warm fat will melt and laminate the flour bits, preventing water from developing the gluten and making the dough sticky and hard to handle. Chilled pieces of fat become thin, irregularly marbled layers after rolling. This is good. This is very good. And it all starts with ice water.

Flour is a hydrophilic substance. It loves water. That means it behaves differently in different climates, with different weather, with age or freshness. Most recipes will tell you to use 5 to 8 tablespoons of water to make pie dough, and to sprinkle the water 1 tablespoon at a time until the dough coheres. This approach puts too much emphasis on measuring—it's impossible to know how much water piecrust really needs until it's had just the right amount, so measurements at this stage are baloney. My method will ask you to pay attention and trust yourself, not your measuring spoons. This might take a little practice, but remember that experience is the best teacher. You'll get the hang of it. Just give your dough everything it asks for and no more.

★ Start with making ice water.

Find a *2-cup liquid measure with a handle and spout* (the classic clear Pyrex measuring pitcher is perfect for this; a teacup is not), *fill it with about 1½ cups of cold water*, and *plop a few ice cubes in.* You will not use that entire amount of water in your pie dough, but it's wise to have extra on hand just in case. Store the pitcher in the freezer while you prepare the next steps of the recipe.

★ Next, measure your flour.

Some people weigh it to ensure the correct amount every time. I use a lazier but just as effective method that sets the tone for the balance of art and science that characterizes this crust-making method.

Using a ½-cup measure, stir the flour to aerate it, then scoop it into a 1-cup measure until a soft mound of flour rises above the cup's rim. Use a bench scraper, a knife, or some other straight edge **to level the flour.** Then dump the cup of flour into your mixing bowl. **Measure 2½ cups** of flour this way. For the last ½ cup, stir the flour well, scoop, and level off.

The idea is to get just the right amount of flour into the bowl without *worrying* about it so much. You're not a flour molecule away from error if you don't get each measurement exactly right. This isn't to say that you should be sloppy with your measurements. Just that the art of pie is to not stress about the details so much that pie-making is no longer a pleasure. Don't worry. Seriously. You're going to make a pie; it's going to be just fine.

★ Add sugar and salt.

You want 1 tablespoon of sugar and 1 teaspoon of salt. I scoop them with measuring spoons, shake the spoons to level them, and toss them into my measured flour. **Kosher salt is best.** It's cheap, it tastes good, and it mixes easily. That said, any kind of neutrally flavored salt will do. If you're making a savory pie, omit the sugar and keep the salt.

Note: It's critical at this point that water gets nowhere near the flour mix. If water touches the flour, the gluten will begin to develop before you're ready. Make sure your bowls and utensils are clean and dry.

★ Add fat (butter, lard, shortening, etc.).

Cut 1 cup of fat into ½- to 1-tablespoon pieces and drop them into your flour. The pieces' size and shape can vary.

Toss the fat with the flour just to coat the pieces. Then gather handfuls of the flour-fat mixture and position your palms up like you're making an offering. (Note: You can use a pastry cutter instead of your hands. It will cut the fat into the flour rather than rub, which is fine. I prefer hands because, with a little practice, you can feel when the dough is ready as well as see when it is ready.) *Rub the fat and flour between your fingers and thumb,* letting the pieces drop back into the bowl. Take another handful, and another, and another, rubbing the fat into the flour with firm, quick movements, dropping the pieces back into the bowl the moment after you've rubbed them. *Make sure to incorporate all the flour,* scooping it up from the bottom and the sides.

You'll notice the flour change from white to very light yellow and from powdery to loosely contained, a texture many cookbooks call "coarse sand." I think it looks closer to cornmeal. *You'll also notice larger pieces of fat. Most should be pea-size, with some almond-size and a couple of cherry-size pieces.* Irregularly sized fat pieces are good; loose, floating flour is not good.

Keep rubbing the mixture until all the flour has been incorporated. You'll begin to smell the fat. That means you're almost done, that your hands have warmed the fat a bit, and that you should stop rubbing very soon. *If the dough feels quite soft, chill it for 5 minutes before moving on to the next step.*

★ Get the water from the freezer.

Pour it over the fat-flour mixture in a thin, steady stream for about 5 seconds. I start *at the edge and spiral inward,* stopping when I get to the center, to make the water easier to distribute evenly. *Then quickly and lightly toss—don't knead!—the flour with your hands until all the water has been distributed.* Toss as you'd toss a salad to distribute oil without smashing delicate vegetables or letting all the heavy stuff fall to the bottom. You may have to toss longer or shorter than you'd expect—go by feel. *When you can't feel any wet spots, stop tossing.*

Pour more water in the same thin spiral. Toss again. And so on. Pebbles of fat will begin to adhere to each other. The texture will change from dry to slightly tacky.

1. Measure the dry ingredients: flour, sugar, and salt.

2. Cut the chilled fat into chunks, then drop them into the flour bowl.

3. Toss the fat with the flour just to coat the pieces, then gather handfuls of the flour-fat mixture.

4. Rub the flour-fat mixture between your fingers and thumb, letting pieces drop back into the bowl.

5. Take another handful, and another, and another, rubbing the flour into the fat with firm, quick movements.

6. After the flour has been incorporated into the fat, pour ice water over the mixture in a thin, steady stream.

7. Toss to distribute the water. Don't knead! When you can't feel any wet spots, stop tossing.

8. Add more water and toss until the texture of the dough changes from dry to slightly tacky and pebbles of fat cling to each other.

9. Scoop up a small amount of the dough, and firmly but gently press it into a ball.

10. Toss it in the air. If it thumps into your hand and keeps its shape, it's done.

11. Gather half of the dough and press it into a thick disk, using your cupped fingers and palms to shape it; repeat with the other half of the dough.

12. Cover the dough in plastic wrap and refrigerate for at least an hour before rolling.

The dough will begin to cling to your fingers (let it, and don't clean your fingers). Toss and pour in quick, light movements until the dough feels slightly tacky.

Scoop up a small amount, firmly but gently press it into a ball, and toss it in the air. If it shatters when it lands in your palm, your dough is too dry. Add more water. *If it thumps into your hand and keeps its shape, it's done.* If the dough feels wet, you've probably added too much water.

When you don't get the water balance just right, I find it's best to follow the advice of *The Victory Binding of the American Woman's Cook Book*: "If too little or too much water has been used, nothing can be done about it, except to profit by experience next time."

★ Shape and store the dough.

Firmly, gently, and quickly gather half the dough and press it into a thick disk, using your cupped fingers and palms to shape it. *Gather the other half* and shape it, too, into a thick disk, using the same method. *Wrap the dough disks individually in plastic wrap and let them rest in the fridge for at least an hour.*

Dough needs to rest for two reasons. One: Right now gluten is like a cranky baby that needs to be put down for a nap. It's tight and spirally and snappy. Not in a good mood. An hour in the fridge will let the proteins relax and prevent them from toughening the dough. Two: Pastry dough is easiest to handle when it has been chilled. *If at any time during the pie-making process you aren't using the dough, it should be in the fridge.* And, if at any point the dough stops behaving and starts sticking or tearing or some other god-awful annoying thing, or if you too are getting frustrated and annoyed, both of you need to chill out. Put the dough in the fridge for 5 to 10 minutes and take a break.

You can refrigerate the dough for up to 3 days. Longer periods will dry it out. Old dough often tastes fine, but it's harder to roll out.

You can also freeze dough for up to one month by first letting it rest in the refrigerator for an hour, then wrapping it tightly in plastic wrap and sealing it in a freezer bag. The dough will be a bit discolored and may be harder to roll out, but it will still be delicious. Defrost frozen dough in the refrigerator before rolling.

This recipe works for all the wheat flour-and-fat recipes that follow.

If you were making your first piecrust and I was in the kitchen with you, and if I saw you worrying and fussing with the dough, I'd lean over your bowl and say, "Stop touching it!" Since I can't be there, I'm going to write it again: stop touching it! You're doing great. Have fun. It's just pie.

❖ HOW TO CHOOSE YOUR BEST TOOLS ❖

Your Hands

The best piecrust is handmade. Anyone who says differently is selling you a food processor. Your hands can sensitively and quickly judge the consistency of the dough; they're easier to clean; and they're the first route through which pie-making becomes a sensual experience. It can be like playing in the mud, but edible.

   A note to those of us who paint our nails: it's best to take the polish off before making dough. One flake can foul the batch.

Things You Hold in Your Hands

ROLLING PIN: My favorite rolling pin is a 1½-inch-thick dowel that I picked up for three bucks when I was having an out-of-town baking emergency. Tapered French pins, straight American-style rollers, hefty marble pins—they all work. Make pie more than once and you'll get a sense for which feels most comfortable in your hand. Use that one. The dowel raises the fewest eyebrows at airport security and is easiest to handle, so it's my traveling as well as my home-game choice.

BENCH SCRAPER: Also called pastry scrapers, bench scrapers are like having an extra, more precise hand. They keep dough from sticking to the rolling surface and help lift rolled-out dough into pie pans. They're important to my crust-making technique and they're cheap, so I'd pick two up if I were you. If you don't have a bench scraper, you can substitute a metal spatula.

KNIFE: There is nothing like a well-sharpened chef's knife. Dull knives are dangerous. Some recipes in this book require very thin fruit slices, in which case you need either a sharp knife or a mandoline. If all you have is a dull knife, skip that recipe.

Measuring Tools

CUPS, SPOONS: I find that with pie, the general rule is ingredients that should be measured with dry measuring cups need to be precise. Ingredients that can be measured with spoons can be fudged a bit.

SPOUTED LIQUID MEASURE: My crust-making method requires a spouted liquid measure or some other measuring cup or pitcher with a spout. I prefer a 2-cup size, as it's easy to handle and contains more water than I really need, which helps me control how much I choose to pour onto the dough.

Bowls

You'll need a set of them. Small, medium, large. Preferably metal, since that chills the best.

Pie Plates

Oh, the glory and variety of American pie plates! Any one description of them will be inaccurate, but I'll try anyway. A pie plate is a rimmed baking dish made of ceramic, glass, or tin that generally measures 9 to 10 inches at the top and 7 to 8 inches at the bottom, is about 2 inches deep, and can hold 4 to 6 cups. The rim is the most important part, the thing that makes a pie pan not just a pan. It cradles the pie's edge so that it sits sturdily and proudly up. The rim might be scalloped or straight. As long as it's there, you can make a pie in that pan.

The best pie plates are ceramic and glass. Aluminum pie pans are useful if you intend to dispose of the pan, but they reflect heat and don't brown the pie as well as ceramic or glass.

My favorites are a red Le Creuset 9-inch ceramic plate, the shallow pink Pyrex 8.75-incher that my father used to make pie for my mother, and a sturdy blue-and-cream 10-inch earthenware deep dish I picked up at the Iowa State Fair. I choose them according to the size of pie I intend to make and whether their textures and colors will be the right frame for the fruit.

A 9-inch pie plate usually holds 4 to 5 cups of fruit. A 10-inch pie plate usually holds 5 to 6 cups of fruit or more, depending on how deep the dishes are.

Cookie Sheets

Useful for catching juice drips. Even more useful if you're making multiple pies at once. For a two-pie job, place the pies evenly spaced on the cookie sheet and slide the sheet into the middle of the oven. Halfway through, rotate the cookie sheet front to back instead of risking third-degree burns with individual pie rotations. Works like a dream for four-pie jobs too—just place two pies on two cookie sheets and bake in the top and bottom of the oven. Halfway through, rotate the sheets front to back and switch the bottom and top sheets to ensure even baking.

Piecrust Shields

Whatever you spend on piecrust shields you save in frustration. They're much easier to work with than aluminum foil and more effective. You can find them wherever you find bench scrapers.

Perch one on the rim of a pie that's beginning to brown too much. It will prevent burning while the rest of the pie bakes. If you don't have a piecrust shield, use foil.

Pie Weights

Anything that can convince a single crust to stay put while blind baking (see "How to Bake Blind," page 49) deserves the name of pie weight. Ceramic weights are best. If you don't have any, use pennies on a sheet of aluminum foil; if you don't have pennies, use beans. I don't suggest the pie "chains" being marketed right now. They're not heavy enough to tame baking dough.

Pie Birds

Are adorable. (See "How to Put a Bird on It," page 52, for more about them.)

Your Senses

Pay attention to what your eyes, ears, nose, mouth, and hands tell you. They're perfectly calibrated for the job.

❧ HOW TO MAKE A DOUBLE-CRUST FRUIT PIE ❧

This section is radically practical. It's about making what you can with what you have. It would rather you pick the filling first and the recipe second, so you don't have to go to the grocery store with an expensive list of ingredients you'll use once and forget about on your pantry shelf. Instead, you'll use what you already have, what's cheap, what's tasty, or what's perfectly ripe right now.

Making what you can with what you have means that you have exactly what you need already, that what you have is enough, that you are enough, and that ultimately you are wiser than this cookbook.

If you're new to pie-making, I suggest first trying out a couple of the more traditional recipes that comprise the rest of the book before moving on to this looser recipe.

Fruit pie filling has five essential ingredients: *fruit, sweetener, salt, spice, and thickener.* Wrap that up in *dough,* and you have a double-crust fruit pie.

★ Fruit

Start with fruit, using what tastes best as your guide. Notice I said *what tastes best* rather than what looks best. Once fruit becomes pie, the beauty contest is over. It's what's inside that counts.

My most successful experiments combine two types of fruit with two different textures and shapes. Peaches and raspberries. Apples and blackberries. Cherry and rhubarb. You can **use as little or as much as you like of any given fruit**—use five different kinds if you like—as long as **the final measurement falls around 5 cups.**

In most pie plates, 4 cups of fruit will make a demure, well-contained treat. Six cups, unless we're talking about apples, will probably end in a fruit drip on the bottom of your oven, which yields a perfectly delicious pie but also a bit of a mess. Five is usually perfect.

The best way to tell how much fruit your pie plate holds is to use the plate itself to measure the fruit. Pile the fruit into the bottom of a clean pie plate until, when leveled, the pile reaches the plate's rim, or just below it. That's the perfect measurement.

Put that fruit into a medium bowl. Time for the second ingredient.

★ Sugar

Midcentury cookbooks (not to mention many modern ones) prefer more. I prefer less. Sweet-tooths, note that if my recipes are too tart for your tastes, you have the power to, as Def Leppard would say, pour some sugar on 'em. **Start with ½ cup.**

Before I go further, let's go back for just a second. I said sugar, but I mean *sweetener.* **Sugar, honey, maple syrup, agave, corn syrup, cane syrup—anything sweet qualifies** and can be used in a pie. When deciding on sweetener, consider the flavor (or lack thereof, as with corn syrup) and if it will add liquid to the final preparation of the pie.

Sugar is our basic sweetener. It's white. It's bright. It's so common that when I think about white sugar, all I think is *sweet*—not, as with brown sugar, *caramel*, or as with honey, *floral*. White sugar gets the job done and gets out of the way. **When you want sweet fruit without too many competing flavors, go with white sugar.** Or use it in combination with another sweetener. Brown sugar and white make a bright caramel-y frame for fruit; honey and white make a floral frame without adding too much liquid to the filling.

Honey is my very favorite sweetener for most fruits. When I say honey, I mean good-quality honey. Not the stuff that comes in plastic bears and has no detectable pollen count. Collect local honey when you travel; get the best, most interestingly flavored kind you can find at the grocery store. **I find that, for pie, a light-flavored floral honey is best.** Buckwheat, lavender, clover, and many unlabeled farmstore-bought varieties have lent subtle and rich flavors to my pies. **To find the best honey, taste it.** Lesser-quality honey just tastes sweet. If you wanted plain sweet, you'd use white sugar. Better-quality honey has a range of flavors that need their own book to be thoroughly described.

Honey is a liquid and, when combined with fruit, often produces very soupy filling. Don't worry. Add a little more thickener to compensate, or reduce the amount of liquid by using half honey, half sugar. **It's also sweeter than sugar, so you can use less. Try ¾ cup honey** instead of 1 cup sugar.

Maple syrup has an easily recognizable, strong flavor. Use it to give fruit a maple flavor, as well as sweeten the pie.

Corn syrup is the least interesting of sweeteners, the sort of sweet that tastes a little hollow underneath, like an empty Coke can. I use it only in emergencies.

The main point for all this sweet talk: like salt, bleach, and mascara, you can always add more later, so go slow. **Evaluate how sweet the fruit is, how sweet your tooth is**, and decide from there. Tart pies with sweet-tart fruit like apricot and plum need about ½ cup of sugar, unless you want a sweet pie. Sweet pies with sweet fruit like peaches need ½ to 1 cup, unless you want a tart pie. Very tart fruit like gooseberries and rhubarb need 1 to 1½ cups sugar. Try blending different sweeteners as you blended different fruits. The only limit is your imagination.

★ Salt

A pinch for every pie. Maybe two. If, once you taste the filling, it still tastes bland, try a little more salt. Salt is a way I judge other people's pie recipes. If it's absent, I'm suspicious.

★ Spice

By spice I mean **fresh and dried spices, herbs, lemon juice, flavor extracts, alcohol,** and anything else you might add to a pie just for fun.

This book errs on the side of less spice. **A pinch of ground nutmeg is often all you need.**

Herbs

Garden herbs like thyme, lemon verbena, basil, lavender, sage, and rosemary can add unexpected sophistication to fruit pie flavors. Start with **1 teaspoon finely chopped herbs** and add from there if needed.

Lemon juice

Many fruits benefit from the acidic zing of lemon juice. Lemon zest, to my taste, does the same thing but is more complicated to produce, so I stick to juice, which requires only strong fingers and a sharp eye for errant seeds. Fresh juice is better, but bottled juice is better than none. Start with the juice of about **half a small lemon (1 tablespoon or so)**. Add more if you want a more pronounced lemon flavor or if the fruit still tastes a little bland. **Lemon's talent is to frame flavors.** You may taste it, but more importantly, it should help you taste the fruit better. This is especially important for super-sweet fruits like strawberries or mild fruit like blueberries.

Extracts

Flavor extracts are fun, but often mask fresh fruit's flavors. Use them to impart a specific flavor, like vanilla or almond, not to heighten the peachiness of a peach.

Alcohol

As for alcohol, those that already taste of baking spices will fare best in a pie. **Whiskey** is phenomenal, especially less-sweet rye whiskies. **Brandy** is another favorite. Fruit-flavored alcohols are better when they contrast with the fruit in the pie. Plum with pear brandy, for example. **Start with 2 tablespoons.** Add another tablespoon to heighten the pie's alcoholic charm. **The booze will bake off**, leaving the flavor.

After you've added the fruit, sweetener, salt, and spice to the mixing bowl, stir gently to combine. Taste the fruit. Is it hard to stop eating? You're done. If it isn't—if it tastes a little plain—a little bland, try adding more lemon, more salt, more spice, more sugar. Whatever it takes, a little bit at a time. When you're happy with the result, add thickener.

★ Thickener

The amount and type of thickener you choose **should depend on the fruit.** First consider pectin content. **Pectin is a natural thickener that exists in the cell walls of fruit.** As fruit ripens, pectin breaks down, causing the fruit to soften. You can extract pectin from the peels and seeds of citrus fruits (which are the source of most commercially sold pectin), and you can use its presence in pie fruit to your advantage.

Apples, pears, and quince have a lot of natural pectin. Because of this, and because of their sturdy, sliceable structure, pie-makers can pile them high and still expect to make a perfectly thickened pie. A grated apple can be used to thicken up a berry pie. Quince is so full of pectin it barely needs thickener at all.

Stone fruits have less pectin. Sour cherries are usually decent sources of it; peaches are not. *Berries are also very low in pectin*, unless we're talking about unripe green gooseberries, which are as sour as rhubarb and, because they're still unripe, are loaded with pectin, hence their former dominance in Britain as a jam thickener.

HIGH PECTIN 5 to 6 cups of fruit will need 2 to 3 tablespoons of thickener	MEDIUM PECTIN 5 to 6 cups of fruit will need 4 to 5 tablespoons of thickener	LOW PECTIN 5 to 6 cups of fruit will need 5 to 6 tablespoons of thickener
Apples	Apricots and apriums	Blackberries and marionberries
Quince	Plums and pluots	Blueberries
Cranberries	Sour cherries	Peaches
Gooseberries	Pears	Raspberries
Lemons (with rind)		Strawberries
		Rhubarb

Another thing to consider: acid content. Acidic fruits can interfere with wheat flour's thickening power. *Use tapioca flour for strawberries, raspberries*, and other high-acid fruits.

If you use wheat flour as a thickener, you must also use a few tablespoons of unsalted butter. As the pie bakes, the flour and butter will combine into a sweet, soft roux. When a pie recipe says "dot the top with butter," it means cut 2 to 3 tablespoons of butter into small pieces and scatter them over the top of flour-coated fruit so that they can combine in the oven's heat.

If you use tapioca flour, sprinkle it on as you stir to prevent clumps from forming.

Tapioca Flour

Tapioca flour is starch extracted from the cassava root—the exact same substance as instant tapioca, tapioca pearls, or the larger tapioca balls found at Asian markets. It's been pulverized to a fine powder that dissolves and thickens pie fillings easily, without the odd gelatinous chunks that can gum up a pie made with larger forms of tapioca. You can make tapioca flour yourself by giving tapioca pearls a whirl in a clean coffee grinder. I prefer to buy tapioca flour already ground from Bob's Red Mill, which is carried by many grocery stores nationwide and can be found online at BobsRedMill.com.

Mix *fruit, sweetener, salt, spice, and thickener* in a medium bowl.

★ Dough

Choose a dough with the right texture and taste for your filling—extra-flaky if you want the dough to pillow the filling in pastry shards, all-butter if you want a sturdier crust, etc. Make it up to 3 days ahead.

Assemble the pie according to the instructions on pages 40 to 43.

Right before baking, brush the top of the crust (but not the rim) with *egg white wash (1 egg white plus one teaspoon water, lightly beaten) or milk* to help it brown, and sprinkle liberally with *sugar* if you wish.

Bake the pie for 10 to 20 minutes at 425 degrees F until blonde and blistered, then lower the heat to 375 degrees F and bake for 35 to 50 minutes more, turning the pie front to back about halfway through cooking to ensure even baking. The pie is done when the crust is golden and juices bubble slowly at the edge.

Cool the pie on a wire rack until it's just barely warm (if you can comfortably touch the bottom of the pie plate, you can serve the pie). Cooling allows the thickener to set up.

You can serve it in wedges with whipped cream, crème fraîche, or ice cream on the side. Or, as I prefer it, by its beautiful lonesome.

❧ HOW TO MAKE A GALETTE ❧

A galette is a free-form, rustic pastry made of all the same parts as pie—crust, filling—but folded instead of shaped and crimped, giving it a ruffled look and cool attitude (see the photos on pages 95 and 152). You can fill it with anything—roasted vegetables, peaches, apples, plums—if it sounds like a good idea, it probably is. With a few minor changes, detailed below, any of the fruit pies in this book can be converted into galettes.

Galettes can be baked in a regular pie dish or cast-iron skillet, or free-form on a parchment-lined baking sheet. Free-form galettes look effortlessly sophisticated, while the cast-iron pan implies frontier cooking, a little dose of Americana in a French-inspired treat.

Galettes keep a firm hold on their fruit when you use less of it—4 cups instead of the 5 or 6 you'd use for a traditional American double-crust pie. Because I'm accustomed to making mile-high American-style pies, I tend to overfill my galettes. The only consequence of this habit worth considering is that the juice bubbles out and caramelizes around the edge of the pan. This is annoying if you're not actually using a pan to bake your galette. But if you are, like me, using a cast-iron skillet, and if you, like me, sprinkle the top of your galette with crunchy sugar, then you are, like me, creating the sweet equivalent of the toasted cheese on the edge of the nacho pan. Otherwise known as the best part.

In a Pan

To make a galette in a pan or pie plate, make the amount of filling described in the pie recipe (or 1 cup less, if you'd like to avoid overfilling the galette) and set aside. Roll out the dough (recipe on page 70) until it's a large round, about ⅛ inch thick. Fold the dough in half, then in half again, and place the corner of the folded dough in the center of the pan. Unfold the dough, tuck it carefully into the edges of the pan, and let the edges drape over the sides.

Free-Form

For a free-form galette, make 4 cups of filling to prevent the galette from excessively seeping fruit juice onto the baking sheet (a little puddling up is okay, and probably unavoidable). Adjust the recipe accordingly, **starting with 4 cups of fruit, ½ cup sweetener, a pinch of salt, a pinch of spice, and a squeeze of lemon.** Taste, adjust the flavors as needed, and add thickener. If you would add 5 tablespoons of flour to a blueberry pie, add 4 to a galette. Two tablespoons of chunked butter (if you're thickening with flour) is still just right. Mix everything and set aside.

Galette recipes that use honey and maple syrup will work best if made in pans, not free-form, to ensure that the galette dough keeps a firm hold on the extra liquid these sweeteners add.

You can **make galette dough up to 3 days ahead.** Use the same handmade method detailed in "How to Make Piecrust by Hand" (page 19). The ingredients and measurements will change and the dough will be a bit wetter, but otherwise galette dough will behave just like pie dough.

When rolling out the galette, use lots of flour on your rolling surface and pin. I roll it out directly on the counter, lifting and turning the dough with a pastry scraper periodically so it doesn't stick. You can also roll it out on parchment paper.

Once the dough is about ⅛ inch thick and in a large round, transfer it to your pie plate or parchment.

Pile the fruit inside, leaving at least 2 or 3 inches of dough around the edges. Pile the filling high, if you can. Form the galette by grabbing part of the edge and folding it gently toward the center until that part of the dough is firmly tucked around the filling, then another edge a little further down the round, bringing that gently toward the center too, continuing around the dough until you've arranged it in an informal ruffle of crust. A window of fruit should shine through the middle.

If the galette sags in one corner or comes undone in another, pinch the dough together where needed to help the galette keep its shape and patch any holes around the bottom to prevent juice from leaking.

Right before baking, brush the ruffled crust with egg white wash and sprinkle it with sugar.

Bake the galette at 450 degrees F for 10 to 15 minutes, or until the crust is blond and blistered. Lower the heat to 350 degrees F (the lower temperature will help keep the exposed fruit from drying out) and bake it for another 35 to 50 minutes. Rotate the galette front to back about halfway through to ensure even baking. The galette is done when the crust is golden and juices from the fruit bubble slowly at the edge of the ruffled crust.

If you baked your galette in a pan, set that pan on a wire rack and let it cool for at least an hour before serving.

If you baked your galette on parchment paper, you can remove the paper by letting the galette cool on the baking sheet for 20 minutes. Then transfer the galette to a wire rack by grabbing the edges of the paper and carefully lifting it onto the rack. Hold the top of the galette gently and pull the parchment paper from beneath it, allowing the bottom to crisp and cool more quickly. Make sure it cools for at least an hour on the rack before serving.

At serving time, gently slide the galette onto a plate or cutting board.

Sometimes I serve the galette from the parchment paper; it looks nearly as rustic as a cast-iron pan.

❖ HOW TO BE A PIE ROLLER ❖

When your dough has sufficiently rested, find a large clean, flat surface, preferably made of wood or marble. A breadboard will do. Sprinkle flour in a large circle over that surface so that it generously clouds it, but not so much that you can't see the surface beneath. You want enough flour to keep the dough from sticking, not so much that you could make another batch. Choose a rolling pin that feels comfortable in your hand. It should be sturdy and just heavy enough to pose a real threat to wannabe pie thieves, but not so heavy that you can't lift it easily over your shoulder.

Remove the plastic wrap from the dough. Lightly flour each side of the disk, set it in the middle of the flour cloud, and give it a good whack with your rolling pin. Whack it again. Turn the dough 90 degrees and whack it a few more times so that the dough evenly flattens. If it splits a little on the outer perimeter, that's okay. You're conditioning the dough, getting it ready to roll.

Roll from the center of the dough to the edge, never back and forth over the entire surface. Keep in mind that by the time you're done rolling, the center will be slightly thicker than the edge. Roll the dough from the center to not-quite-the-edge to keep the thickness even. After three or four rolls, slide a bench scraper underneath the dough to unstick it from the surface. Turn the dough 90 degrees. Roll again. Turn again. By scraping and turning, you'll have an easier time rolling the dough into a round shape.

While you're rolling, flour as needed to keep the dough from sticking to the rolling pin and rolling surface.

When the dough is about 12 inches in diameter, use the bench scraper to unstick it from the counter. Slide it as far under the dough as you can; put your other hand on the top side of the dough so it's gently held on both sides; and flip the whole thing over. Continue to roll it out from center to edge, turning it as you go, until the dough is ⅛ inch thick.

To combat any cracks, roll firmly but slowly, in small, brief motions, over both sides of the crack, stopping just short of rolling over the crack. The two sides will grow closer together—if not completely together—either fixing the

1. Lightly flour each side of a disk of dough, set it on a floured surface, and give it a good whack with your rolling pin.

2. Roll from the center of the dough to the edge until the dough is a large round, about ⅛ inch thick. As you roll, turn the dough often to help it form an even round and prevent it from sticking to the rolling surface.

3. Slide a bench scraper underneath the dough to unstick it from the rolling surface.

4. With the bench scraper, quickly fold the dough in half. Fold it again into quarters.

5. Place the point of the folded dough in the middle of your pie dish.

6. Unfold the dough over the pie dish, tuck it gently into the corners of the dish, and trim the edge so it hangs only 1 inch off the rim of the plate.

dough or making a patch job easier. (Wait to patch your unruly dough until it's in the pie plate: trim the edges and use those to patch up any remaining cracks.)

To transfer the dough to the pie plate, slide a bench scraper underneath it to unstick it from the rolling surface. Then slide the bench scraper as far as you can beneath an edge of the dough and quickly, confidently (fake it until you make it) fold the dough in half. Fold it again. Now your dough is in quarters, with the middle of the dough conveniently folded into a point. Place that point in the middle of your pie dish and unfold the dough.

Quickly, confidently. Tuck it gently into the corners of the pan. Don't stretch the dough! It has a memory; it will bounce back.

Trim the dough's edges so they hang only 1 inch off the edge of the plate. Too much overhang will create too big of a folded edge, which may not bake all the way through. Don't tuck this overhang into the plate just yet; wait for the top crust.

Place the bottom crust in the refrigerator while you prepare the filling and top crust.

Roll out the top crust the same way you rolled out the bottom crust. While the top crust is folded in quarters, try cutting designs into it as you would a paper snowflake, making cuts or half-shapes at the folded edges of the dough so that when you unfold it over the pie, full shapes and V's appear, providing decoration and ventilation.

Place the point of the quarter-folded top crust in the center of the pie filling and unfold the crust over the top of the pie. Trim the crust so it hangs only 1 inch over the edge of the pie plate. Create a folded edge by tucking both layers of pastry into the pie plate. Crimp with your fingers or use the tines of a fork to make a decorative edge.

Cut large vents, if you haven't already cut them, into the top crust, brush the top crust with egg white wash (but not the edges, which will brown before the rest of the pie), sprinkle with sugar, and bake according to the recipe's instructions.

1. Center your top crust by placing the point of the folded dough in the center of the filled pie.

2. Unfold the crust over the pie.

3. Trim the crust so it hangs only 1 inch over the edge of the pie plate.

4. Create a folded edge by tucking both layers of pastry into the pie plate.

5. Fold the edge, don't pinch, into place.

6. Crimp with your fingers to make a decorative edge.

❖ HOW TO BE FRUITFUL ❖

Choose the best fruit that's in season. Every time. If nothing is in season (or it's August and you have a craving for rhubarb), choose fruit that has been frozen with no additives (like sugar). If you can taste the fruit, taste it. I hate it when I go home with a bag of gorgeous peaches only to find out they taste like soft chalk. Use ripe fruit always. Unripe fruit isn't improved by baking nearly as much as you'd hope.

Most pies call for 5 to 6 cups of fruit. Some people weigh their fruit with a scale to get more exact proportions. I prefer to eyeball it one of two ways. The first is to place sliced fruit or raw berries in a large liquid measuring pitcher. No need to squish them down to eliminate air holes—just place the fruit gently in the pitcher and pile it up until you're at or slightly above the measurement line. Another way to measure fruit is to fit it exactly to your pie plate. Pile cut fruit into the plate until it's level (or a little below) the rim of the plate. That amount will work best for that plate. Keep in mind that if you're using a large deep-dish plate, you'll be able to fit more fruit into the pie than the recipe may call for. If that's the case, add a little more sugar and thickener. If a recipe calls for ¼ cup tapioca, for example, I'll add another tablespoon or use a heaping ¼ cup.

Apples, pears, and quince are an exception to this rule of measurement. Because of their firm textures and high pectin content, you can pile thin slices of them much higher than the rim of the plate without worrying the pie will juice all over the oven. Again, if you decide to use more fruit than the recipe calls for, adjust sugar, seasoning, and thickener to match the larger quantity.

Pie juices like to drip, burn, smoke, and gum up the bottom of your oven. Save yourself some elbow grease by baking the pie on a baking sheet. The only time I don't do this is when I'm baking in a gas oven that doesn't have a convection setting. The sheet can interfere with even heat distribution.

A note on thickeners: Acidic fruits can neutralize the thickening power of flour and butter, so use tapioca flour for acidic berries instead. Quick-cooking tapioca pearls work too, but I prefer the consistent texture of tapioca flour. Cornstarch is a perfectly good thickener, but I don't like the way it tastes so I don't use it in my fruit pies.

The best pies use the best fruit. It's as simple as that. If I can't find decent fruit, I don't make pie. Or I make a winter pie—pumpkin (which tastes as good from a can as it does fresh), pecan, or some other sugary, seasonless concoction.

❖ HOW TO KEEP YOUR COOL ❖

Let's talk about frozen fruit. It's the best way to keep high-quality fruit year-round. You don't need to defrost the fruit, but you can. In some cases, like with marionberries, you can achieve better textures when you use frozen instead of fresh. In others, like peaches, the frozen fruit might make a soupy pie, so it's best to defrost them in a sieve and use the juice for something else, ice cream or cocktails, for example. When using frozen fruit, let the filling sit in its mixing bowl for an extra 15 minutes after you've made it. If you're baking a frozen pie, assume that the baking time will need to increase by 10 to 20 minutes (sometimes even 30).

I prefer to freeze my own fresh fruit during the summer or find a steady high-quality supply in my grocery's freezer aisle. Freezing premade pie filling and premade pies are worthy options too, the only drawback being, to my taste, that premade frozen pies are not quite as good as pies made with fresh crust and frozen fruit. But they're 200 percent better than no pie at all. Especially when the only fresh produce you've eaten for months is kale.

If fruit has been flash-frozen, let it thaw for about fifteen minutes before using it in filling. Freezing helps many fruits keep their shape during the mixing and baking process, but fully frozen fruits sometimes slow down baking times.

A trick to creating prize-winning texture: while the fruit is frozen, smash it up a bit with a wooden spoon, just enough that the broken bits cradle the whole bits, so you have neither jam (as you might with fresh berries) nor wholly independent pieces of fruit rolling around the plate.

If fruit hasn't been flash-frozen (i.e., you froze it yourself) and it appears to be a huge chunk of unstirrable fruit ice, set the block in a sieve, put the sieve over a bowl, and allow it to thaw almost completely before using, collecting the juice for a different purpose. You can stop thawing when the fruit is soft enough to combine easily with other ingredients.

To freeze pie dough, make it, refrigerate it for an hour (so the dough can properly rest before its deep sleep), wrap it tightly in plastic wrap, and seal it in a freezer bag or container. Thaw frozen dough in the refrigerator, not on the counter.

To freeze a whole pie, first let the freshly constructed but still raw pie sit in the freezer for 15 to 20 minutes, or until the dough is quite firm. Then wrap the pie in plastic wrap and seal it in a gallon-size freezer bag or a large plastic container (old Tupperware cake carriers are perfect for this purpose and are easy enough to find at Goodwill). Do not thaw; just bake it frozen at the temperatures indicated in the original recipe. Anticipate that each stage of baking will very likely be longer. Judge doneness by sight rather than by timer.

Bake frozen dough and frozen pie within one month of freezing for the best quality.

To freeze pie filling, make the filling according to the recipe's instructions (fruit, sugar, salt, spice, thickener: about 5 to 6 cups total) and freeze in gallon-size freezer bags. To use, first allow it to thaw enough to be easily mounded into a pie shell.

❖ HOW TO BAKE ❖

No matter how well a cookbook is written, the cooking times it gives will be wrong. Ingredients don't take three or five or ten minutes to be done; it depends on the day and the stove. So you must simply pay attention, trust yourself, and decide.

—TAMAR ADLER, AN EVERLASTING MEAL

Sometimes the early pie-baking process is described as "tempering the dough." The face, but not the edges, of an unbaked pie is brushed with egg white wash and set in the middle of an oven that has in turn been set at a high temperature, 425 or 450 degrees F. The heat "shocks" the crust, rapidly evaporating the water in the dough so the dough keeps its shape. All this vocabulary sounds a bit like we're making something out of metal, a sword or a horseshoe or something that lifts heavy things. Logically the metaphor doesn't fit, yet it feels completely appropriate.

If you were to keep the oven that hot, the pie would burn before it baked. Once the crust has "annealed," it looks blond and blistered and a little dry, not melty or translucent or, on the other end of the spectrum, brown. Now you can turn the oven down to 375 or 350 degrees F. For pies whose fruit is mostly covered by a crust, I choose a 425/375 combination. For open-faced pies like galettes, where high heat might dry out or sear the fruit, I prefer a 450/350 combination. The final baking time (the sum of the high and low baking times) is around an hour for both combinations of temperatures—10 to 20 minutes longer if you've used frozen fruit (see page 45).

Set a timer for the minimum time range specified and check on the pie when the timer goes off. If the pie doesn't look blond and blistered, check on it again in 5 minutes. And again in 5 minutes, if that's what it takes. Don't reduce the heat until the pie looks like it's ready for a lower temperature, and be careful not to leave the oven door open for too long.

The same goes for the second half of the baking process, when the lower heat cooks the fruit and thickens its juices. If the fruit/thickener balance is right, the pie isn't done until the juice bubbles slowly at the edges. You'll see the bubbles change from bright and watery to a lazy, viscous burble. The crust will be a golden brown.

Halfway through baking, turn the pie front to back so the crust browns evenly. If at any time during the baking process the crust starts to look too dark, like it might burn, protect those spots with aluminum foil or a piecrust shield.

If the fruit was too juicy for the amount of thickener added, the juices will never quite thicken up. You'll know this is happening when the pie has been in the oven for over an hour, the crust is clearly done (perhaps getting a little too brown), and the juices are still bubbling merrily, maybe pooled around the edges and sogging up the top crust a bit. When that happens, there's nothing to be done. Take the pie out of the oven before the crust burns and let it cool before cutting it. The juices may spill all over the plate, ruining the aesthetic effect of the "perfect" pie, but the crust and fruit will still be delicious. Only a fool would refuse a slice.

❖ HOW TO BAKE BLIND ❖

"Blind" baking means bake the crust bare, without filling. Handy for custard, chiffon, and fresh fruit pies that don't belong anywhere near an oven but need a sturdy crust to stretch out in.

Blind baking is simple if you have a hot oven and a jar of ceramic weights. If your oven has cool spots (for example, near the door), the crust will slump wherever it hits that spot. If you blind bake without pie weights, your crust will puff and balloon and then slump.

Both disasters remain delicious. I've made quiche in a single crust with terrible posture that perked up when I drowned it in eggs and cheese. The oven fused everything into a delicious (though unphotogenic) breakfast.

Here's what you'll need:

★ dough for a single-crust pie

★ a pie plate

★ ceramic pie weights (or pennies or beans)

★ aluminum foil

★ a fork

Roll out the dough, slip it into the pie plate, tuck it in, trim it. Fold and crimp the edge.

Freeze it while you preheat your oven to 425 degrees F.

Freezing the dough briefly before baking helps it maintain its shape. You want to shock the crust, sort of like a hot-to-cold dunking at a Russian spa. Water will evaporate and puff out the fat/flour matrix you've developed in the dough, leaving flakes and a decorative edge with near-perfect military posture.

When the oven is ready, retrieve the dough from the freezer. Dock the bottom and sides with your fork by pressing the tines into the dough and twisting just a little. These holes will let steam and air escape, which will keep the dough from billowing up. Line the crust with aluminum foil so the edges of the foil stick up (don't fold them over the crust) and fill the foil with pie weights (or pennies, or beans). These weights help the dough stay in place along the sides and bottom.

Bake the crust in the center of the oven at 425 degrees F for 10 to 15 minutes. When the crust looks blistered and blond, remove it from the oven and turn the heat down to 375 degrees F. The foil will cool immediately, allowing you to pick it and all the weights up and out of the crust. Put the empty piecrust back into the oven and bake for another 15 to 20 minutes, or until the bottom looks dry and slightly golden, and the edges are a little brown.

Cool on a wire rack before filling.

❧ HOW TO WEAVE A CLASSIC LATTICE ❧

To make a lattice crust, cut the top crust into strips with a pizza or ravioli cutter. Strips can be any size you wish—I usually cut 1-inch strips, though four large strips or strips of various sizes can look neat. Weave the strips by placing one near the edge of the pie plate, then another perpendicular to that strip. Place another strip parallel to the first and weave it under. Place another strip parallel to the second and weave it under where needed to create a woven lattice pattern. Keep up this pattern, alternating the sides you place the strips, weaving as needed until the pie is covered with a lattice. Trim the edges so they're no longer than 1 inch over the pie pan's rim and tuck them under to form a folded edge. Flute if you want to.

1. Cut the top crust into strips.

2. Place one strip near the edge of the pie plate, then place another at the pie's edge perpendicular to that strip.

3. Place another strip parallel to the first and weave it under. Place another strip parallel to the second and weave it under where needed to create a woven lattice pattern.

4. Alternate sides as you place strips and weave as you go until the pie is covered with a lattice.

5. Trim the edges so they hang only 1 inch over the rim of the pie plate.

6. Tuck the edges into the plate to form a folded edge.

❧ HOW TO PUT A BIRD ON IT ❧

Pie birds are hollow, ceramic, bird-shaped funnels that are as useful as they are beautiful. Antique pie birds can cost a pretty penny, and often aren't fit for oven use anymore. Leave those on your knickknack shelf and try newfangled old-looking pie birds instead. They capture steam from baking fruit and funnel it out of the pie, ensuring that your fruit is baking, not braising.

To use a pie bird, nestle it into the center of the filling before putting on the top crust. While the top crust is folded in quarters, snip about an inch off the tip. Unfold the crust around the bird so that the hole in the middle settles around the bird. Trim and crimp as usual. If the filling is juicy, cut extra vents in the top crust. Bake according to the recipe instructions.

❧ HOW TO BE SCRAPPY ❧

All the dough recipes in this book will make slightly more dough than you need, leaving you with crescents and strips of unused, unbaked dough after you've trimmed the bottom and top crusts. There are many easy ways to turn these scraps into a pre-dessert dessert. You could bake them as is, or brush them with egg white wash and sugar, or save them in a ball to roll out later. I once heard a deli secret from a friend whose job it was to roll rugelach, the Jewish version of this treat: roll the dough in powdered sugar, not flour, to add another layer of sweetness.

Some scrappy ideas:

1. Spread scraps on a baking sheet as if they were cookies, paint them with egg white wash or milk, and sprinkle them with spices and sugar (cinnamon sugar is the classic choice). Bake the scraps at 375 degrees F for 15 to 20 minutes, until golden. Eat hot off the tray if you like, or allow to cool before shuffling them from tray to plate with a spatula.

1. *Pie birds funnel steam from baking fruit pies.*

2. *Nestle a pie bird into the center of a filled pie.*

3. *Roll out and fold the top crust in quarters.*

4. *Snip the tip off the folded crust.*

5. *Unfold the crust around the bird.*

6. *Trim and crimp as usual.*

2. Gather the scraps into a ball. As you make scraps, add them to the ball. When the dough ball is about the size of a regular pie dough disk, roll it out to an ⅛-inch thickness, cut them into strips and twist, or make shapes with cookie cutters. Spread the dough shapes on a baking sheet, paint them with egg white wash or milk, and sprinkle them with spices and sugar. Bake at 375 degrees F for 15 to 20 minutes, until golden.

3. After rolling the dough scraps out, paint the dough with egg white wash, and sprinkle it liberally with spices and sugar. Roll the dough into a long tube, like a jelly roll, and slice it width-wise into 1- to 2-inch cookies, so a spiral of the spiced sugar appears. Bake them laying down at 375 degrees F, like cookies, so that the filling doesn't smush out during baking, about 20 minutes, until golden.

❧ HOW TO MULTIPLY ❧

David Mamet says, "Stress cannot exist in the presence of pie." Clearly he's never been in charge of baking a pie buffet.

There are a few tricks to staying cool during a pie-baking bonanza. I learned them from experience, which is to say I've had my share of meltdowns.

★ Some people would choose to let their food processors rescue them from extra dough-making labor. I still use my hands. I have the best luck with doubling a dough recipe rather than tripling or quadrupling.

★ When working with a lot of dough it's helpful to weigh each disk rather than eyeball them to make sure they're the right size. Eight to ten ounces of dough will roll out just right for large pie dishes, seven to eight ounces for smaller dishes.

★ Open-faced or crumble-top pies are less labor overall. Multiply the crumble recipe as many times for as many pies as you're making, make the crumble, and refrigerate it until you're ready to sprinkle it on.

A challenge of baking multiple pies at once is having all the pies ready to bake at the same time. Preparing part of a batch long before the rest of the batch gives the filling time to sog up the unbaked pie crust beneath it. If your unbaked pie sits on the counter for too long, you court disaster and disappointment. This order of tasks gets the timing right most of the time:

★ Make the dough for your batch (conventional ovens fit one to four pies).

★ While the dough rests in the refrigerator, make the filling. Set the filling aside.

★ Preheat the oven to 425 degrees F, or whatever the recipe specifies.

★ Roll out a bottom crust, fit it into the plate, and trim it. Store it in the refrigerator while you roll out the rest of the crusts. Repeat this step as many times as necessary to make the number of pies you're making.

★ Roll out a top crust. Fold in fourths and, still folded, place it lightly in a dough-lined plate in the refrigerator so both crusts will be ready when you need them. Repeat until you've made all the top crusts.

★ Remove one dough-lined plate from the refrigerator. Remove the top crust from the plate, and set it on a cool clean surface near you. Retrieve a bottom crust from the fridge and fill the pie with filling. Retrieve the top crust, place it over the pie, trim and crimp the edges, and cut vents. Store the pie in the refrigerator and repeat these instructions with the next pie.

★ Place unbaked pies on parchment-lined baking sheets.

★ Brush all top crusts with egg white wash and sprinkle with sugar.

★ Bake pies on parchment-lined cookie sheets in pairs, as evenly spaced in the oven as possible. For many ovens, uneven heating will be an issue. Rotate the pies halfway through baking by grabbing the cookie sheet with an oven mitt and rotating the sheet, with the pies on it, instead of risking burns by rotating pies individually. If you're baking four pies, try to get those pies as evenly spaced in the oven as possible—one pair will be close to the top, one to the bottom. To prevent scorching and underbaking, turn the pies 180 degrees *and* switch them from top to bottom halfway through baking.

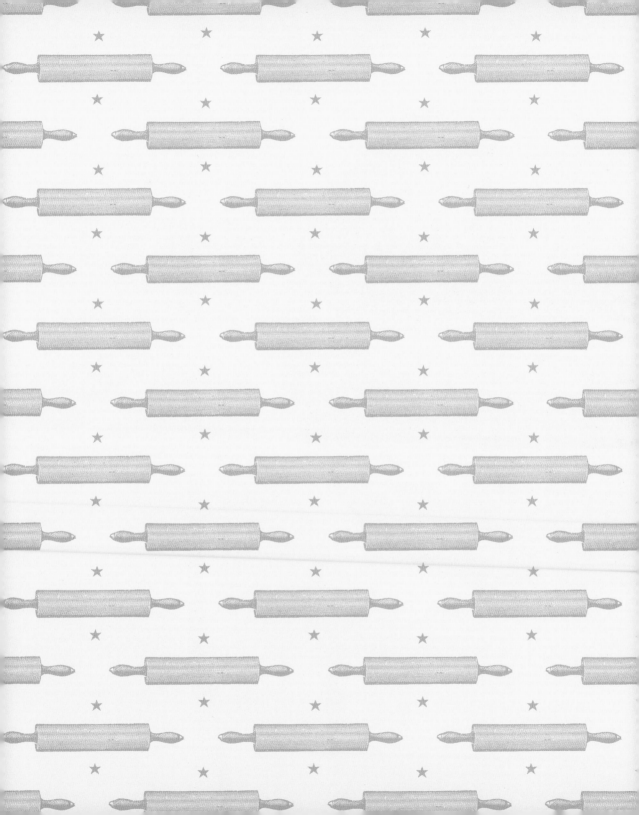

what makes a pie a pie

(OR, RECIPES FOR PIECRUST)

Perfect American piecrust must be seven things at once—flaky, airy, light, tender, crisp, well browned, and good tasting. The tricky ones are flaky, tender, and crisp—because these are independent virtues. Getting flaky, tender, and crisp to happen at the same time in the same pie seems nearly impossible. Yet millions of American women and men in the early 1900s could do it in their sleep, and probably tens of thousands can today.

—JEFFREY STEINGARTEN, THE MAN WHO ATE EVERYTHING

★ ★ ★ ★ ★

Pie, like any good dish, unfolds like an event. For those who think anticipation is the sweetest form of pleasure, the event starts the moment they see the pie warm and golden on its cooling rack, or hear the word *pie* like a promise, or start salivating when they read those three letters on a diner menu. For those of us who don't believe patience is a virtue, the event starts with the first bite, perfectly triangular and composed on our forks. I'm not sure anyone thinks bites from the middle are best, for that's when we are satisfied *and* hungry, a confusing state that makes most of us rush each bite with the next and the next, until we get to the best part.

And what might that be? The finale, of course. The crust. If you eat from point to edge like I do, crust is the best, richest, and sweetest part—not just because it is full of butter, but because it signals that dessert is almost over.

❧ EXTRA-FLAKY PIECRUST ❧

This recipe produces dough that's a dream to roll out (often on the first try!) and a breeze to crimp. Once baked, it's flaky enough to shatter on a fork, yet sturdy enough to hold its shape on the plate. It's the bane of my vegetarian friends, who usually wish I hadn't told them about the lard. My excuse—"It's the meat you can't see!"—hasn't, so far, been convincing. Too bad. More pie for the meat eaters.

Makes 1 double crust

1. Fill a spouted liquid measuring cup with about 1½ cups of water, plop in some ice cubes, and place it in the freezer while you prepare the next steps of the recipe. The idea is to have more water than you need for the recipe (which will probably use ½ cup or less) at a very cold temperature, not to actually freeze the water or use all 1½ cups in the dough.

2. In a large bowl, mix the flour, sugar, and salt. Cut ½- to 1-tablespoon pieces of butter and lard and drop them into the flour. Toss the fat with the flour to evenly distribute it.

3. Position your hands palms up, fingers loosely curled. Scoop up flour and fat and rub it between your thumb and fingers, letting it fall back into the bowl after rubbing. Do this, reaching into the bottom and around the sides to incorporate all the flour into the fat, until the mixture is slightly yellow, slightly damp. It should be chunky—mostly pea-size with some almond- and cherry-size pieces. The smaller bits should resemble coarse cornmeal.

continued

2½ cups flour

1 tablespoon sugar

1 teaspoon salt

½ cup (1 stick) well-chilled unsalted butter

½ cup well-chilled leaf lard (see page 63)

4. Take the water out of the freezer. Pour it in a steady thin stream around the bowl for about 5 seconds. Toss to distribute the moisture. You'll probably need to pour a little more water on and toss again. As you toss and the dough gets close to perfection, it will become a bit shaggy and slightly tacky to the touch. Press a small bit of the mixture together and toss it gently in the air. If it breaks apart when you catch it, add more water, toss to distribute the moisture, and test again. If the dough ball keeps its shape, it's done. (When all is said and done, you'll have added about ⅓ to ½ cup water.)

5. With firm, brief pressure, gather the dough into 2 roughly equal balls (if one is larger, use that for the bottom crust). Quickly form the dough into thick disks using your palms and thumbs. Wrap the disks individually in plastic wrap. Refrigerate for an hour to 3 days before rolling.

on lard

Lard got a bad rap from Industrial Era vegetable shortening ads. Jingles like "the stomach welcomes Crisco" took advantage of the public outcry inspired by Upton Sinclair's *The Jungle*, where a factory worker disappears into a vat of lard, never to be seen again. Distrust of lard coincided with a surplus of canola oil created when Thomas Edison's pesky lightbulb gutted the candle market. Food scientists came to the candle industry's rescue. They could hydrogenate that oil and sell it as a light, pure, and healthy alternative to pig fat. All they had to do was convince the public their fat was safer, cleaner, healthier.

If lard isn't having its day as you read this, it's about to. Now public outcry is obsessed with triglycerides and "fake" foods, including previously sinless substances like Crisco. Lard is a nostalgic, "natural" source of fat that has no equal when it comes to pastry flavor and texture. Bring on the lard!

Like vegetable shortening, lard is a champion of flake in pie dough. It has less water, so it activates gluten less, and it has a higher boiling temperature than butter, so lard crusts hold their shape a bit better than butter crusts. Unlike shortening, which is mostly tasteless, lard is delicious, with a sweet, mysteriously satisfying taste and scent that makes this piecrust my very, very favorite.

But don't buy just any lard. Get leaf lard. It's a purer fat that pads a pig's kidneys, called "leaf" because of the way it shears off in leaves as it's gathered. Cheaper lards taste and smell like pork. Maybe a good idea for savory pie, not so much for sweet pies. Toxins accumulate in fat, so go organic if you can. Get high-quality leaf lard at butcher shops.

❖ ALL-BUTTER PIECRUST ❖

In pursuit of "perfect" piecrust, some recipes advocate for this secret ingredient or that. Vinegar, maybe (which slows down gluten formation), an egg (which adds protein to the dough, binding it together and making it easier to roll), or even vodka (which evaporates during baking without having developed wheat flour's gluten). These additives are especially useful when you're making piecrust in a food processor, which can work the hell out of the crust with one pulse too many.

But they aren't necessary. Not when you're making dough by hand. With my method, this all-butter crust recipe creates a dough that's as tender as it is flaky, which means it's not going to explode into shards like a puff pastry when you take a bite. Rather, it will frame the filling in rich, light pastry layers that are strong enough for you to pick up a slice and eat it by hand.

This crust is so easy to work with, its ingredients so easy to find and store, I use it in all my pie classes. When making pie for myself, it's the recipe I lean on like an old friend.

Makes 1 double crust

2½ cups flour

1 tablespoon sugar

1 teaspoon salt

1 cup (2 sticks) well-chilled
  unsalted butter

1. Fill a spouted liquid measuring cup with about 1½ cups of water, plop in some ice cubes, and place it in the freezer while you prepare the next steps of the recipe. The idea is to have more water than you need for the recipe (which will probably use ½ cup or less) at a very cold temperature, not to actually freeze the water or use all 1½ cups in the dough.

2. In a large bowl, mix the flour, sugar, and salt. Cut ½- to 1-tablespoon pieces of butter and drop them into the flour. Toss the fat with the flour to evenly distribute it.

3. Position your hands palms up, fingers loosely curled. Scoop up flour and fat and rub it between your thumb and fingers, letting it fall back into the bowl after rubbing. Do this, reaching into the bottom and around the sides to incorporate all the flour into the fat, until the mixture is slightly yellow, slightly damp. It should be chunky—mostly pea-size with some almond- and cherry-size pieces. The smaller bits should resemble coarse cornmeal.

4. Take the water out of the freezer. Pour it in a steady thin stream around the bowl for about 5 seconds. Toss to distribute the moisture. You'll probably need to pour a little more water on and toss again. As you toss and the dough gets close to perfection, it will become a bit shaggy and slightly tacky to the touch. Press a small bit of the mixture together and toss it gently in the air. If it breaks apart when you catch it, add more water, toss to distribute the moisture, and test again. If the dough ball keeps its shape, it's done. (When all is said and done, you'll have added about ⅓ to ½ cup water.)

5. With firm, brief pressure, gather the dough in 2 roughly equal balls (if one is larger, use that for the bottom crust). Quickly form the dough into thick disks using your palms and thumbs. Wrap the disks individually in plastic wrap. Refrigerate for an hour to 3 days before rolling.

❖ PURPLE-RIBBON PIECRUST ❖

The first time I entered a pie contest I dropped my pie off at the door and ran home, utterly convinced I was a fool for trying. But I won. As in, the entire contest: Best in Show, purple ribbon, the whole enchilada. This butter-and-shortening crust stole the show because it's flaky from center to edge and flavorful, not because it's beautiful. If your fresh-baked pie looks a bit homely, you're doing it right.

Makes 1 double crust

2½ cups flour

1 tablespoon sugar

1 teaspoon salt

12 tablespoons (1½ sticks) well-chilled unsalted butter

½ cup well-chilled vegetable shortening

1. Fill a spouted liquid measuring cup with about 1½ cups of water, plop in some ice cubes, and place it in the freezer while you prepare the next steps of the recipe. The idea is to have more water than you need for the recipe (which will probably use ½ cup or less) at a very cold temperature, not to actually freeze the water or use all 1½ cups in the dough.

2. In a large bowl, mix the flour, sugar, and salt. Cut tablespoon-size pieces of butter and shortening and drop them into the flour. Toss the fat with the flour to evenly distribute it.

3. Position your hands palms up, fingers loosely curled. Scoop up flour and fat and rub it between your thumb and fingers, letting it fall back into the bowl after rubbing it. Do this, reaching into the bottom and around the sides to incorporate all the flour into the fat, until the mixture is slightly yellow, slightly damp. It should be chunky—mostly pea-size with some almond- and cherry-size pieces. The smaller bits should resemble coarse cornmeal.

4. Take the water out of the freezer. Pour it in a steady thin stream around the bowl for about 5 seconds. Toss to distribute the moisture. You'll probably need to pour a little more water on and toss again. As you toss and the dough gets close to perfection, it will become a bit shaggy and slightly tacky to the touch. Press a small bit of the mixture together and toss it gently in the air. If it breaks apart when you catch it, add more water, toss to distribute the moisture, and test again. If the dough ball keeps its shape, it's done. (When all is said and done, you'll have added about ⅓ to ½ cup water.)

5. With firm, brief pressure, gather the dough in 2 roughly equal balls (if one is larger, use that for the bottom crust). Quickly form the dough into thick disks using your palms and thumbs. Wrap the disks individually in plastic wrap. Refrigerate for an hour to 3 days before rolling.

Shortening is quite soft when refrigerated, which can make this dough slightly more difficult to roll out. Unless I am patient and slow with the rolling pin, the dough often ends up with a hole in the middle. If that happens to you, don't fret. Put the hole-y dough in the pie plate, place the edges of the hole together as best you can without folding or otherwise marring the rest of the dough, and patch any leftover holes with pieces from the edge.

The extra ¼ cup of fat (when compared to my other dough recipes) means there is usually plenty of dough left over. When I double this recipe, I usually get two and a half double crusts (or five single crusts).

❖ CHEESE CRUST ❖

Use any cheese that's hard enough to grate. Cheddar is always a good choice. Gruyère and smoked Gouda are also delicious.

You'd be surprised how difficult it is to tell an unbaked cheese dough from plain unbaked dough, so if you're making more than one kind of crust, label them. Or be prepared for delicious accidents.

Makes 1 double crust

2½ cups flour

1 teaspoon salt

1 cup (2 sticks) well-chilled unsalted butter

1 cup grated sharp cheddar, smoked Gouda, Gruyère, or some other hard-ish, flavorful cheese

1. Fill a spouted liquid measuring cup with about 1½ cups of water, plop in some ice cubes, and place it in the freezer while you prepare the next steps of the recipe. The idea is to have more water than you need for the recipe (which will probably use ½ cup or less) at a very cold temperature, not to actually freeze the water or use all 1½ cups in the dough.

2. In a large bowl, mix the flour and salt. Cut ½- to 1-tablespoon pieces of butter and drop them into the flour. Toss the fat with the flour to evenly distribute it.

3. Position your hands palms up, fingers loosely curled. Scoop up flour and fat and rub it between your thumb and fingers, letting it fall back into the bowl after rubbing. Do this, reaching into the bottom and around the sides to incorporate all the flour into the fat until the mixture is slightly yellow, slightly damp. It should be chunky—mostly pea-size with some almond- and cherry-size pieces. The smaller bits should resemble coarse cornmeal. Toss the cheese with the dough until it is evenly distributed.

4. Take the water out of the freezer. Pour it in a steady thin stream around the bowl for about 5 seconds. Toss to distribute the moisture. You'll probably need to pour a little more water on and toss again. As you toss and the dough gets close to perfection, it will become a bit shaggy and slightly tacky to the touch. Press a small bit of the mixture together and toss it gently in the air. If it breaks apart when you catch it, add more water, toss to distribute the moisture, and test again. If the dough ball keeps its shape, it's done. (When all is said and done, you'll have added about ⅓ to ½ cup water.)

5. With firm, brief pressure, gather the dough in 2 roughly equal balls (if one is larger, use that for the bottom crust). Quickly form the dough into thick disks using your palms and thumbs. Wrap the disks individually in plastic wrap. Refrigerate for an hour to 3 days before rolling.

❖ GALETTE DOUGH ❖

Galettes are a fast and sophisticated route to dinner or dessert. Fast because you can forget the precision of crimping and fluting edges; sophisticated for no other reason than they're French. The crust bakes up tender or flaky, depending on how much liquid you mix into the dough, and it's tarted up with sour cream or cream cheese, which makes a rich frame for simple fillings.

If you use all the liquid the recipe calls for, the dough is wetter, more pliable, easier to handle, and harder to mess up than American-style pie dough, so it's great for new pie-makers. If you're short on time and patience, give a galette a try.

Makes 1 galette crust

¼ cup sour cream or room temperature cream cheese (see note, page 71)

1 tablespoon freshly squeezed lemon juice

¼ cup cold water

1¼ cups all-purpose flour

½ teaspoon salt

½ cup (1 stick) well-chilled butter

1. Whisk the sour cream, lemon juice, and water in a 2-cup spouted liquid measuring cup and put it in the freezer while you prepare the next steps of the recipe. The idea is to have the liquid at a very cold temperature, not to actually freeze it.

2. In a medium bowl, mix the flour and salt. Cut the butter into ½- to 1-tablespoon-size pieces and drop them into the flour. Toss the fat with the flour to evenly distribute it.

3. Position your hands palms up, fingers loosely curled. Scoop up flour and fat and rub it between your thumb and fingers, letting it fall back into the bowl after rubbing. Do this, reaching into the bottom and around the sides to incorporate all the flour into the fat until the mixture is slightly yellow, slightly damp. It should be chunky—mostly pea-size with a handful of almond-size pieces and a few the size of cherries. The rest of the flour/butter mixture should look like coarse cornmeal.

4. Take the liquid out of the freezer. Pour it in a steady thin stream around the bowl for about 5 seconds. Toss everything lightly a few times. If you'd like a flakier crust, stop adding liquid when the dough just coheres. If you'd like a tender crust, pour most of the rest of the liquid in a thin stream over the dough, each time stopping after about 5 seconds to toss and distribute the liquid. The dough should hold together (no puffs of dry flour) and feel a little wet. Expect it to feel much wetter than pie dough, but not so wet that it's like batter. The dough should hold together easily in a ball. Add the rest of the liquid, if needed.

5. With firm, brief pressure, gather the dough into a ball. Quickly form the dough into a thick disk using your palms and thumbs. Wrap it in plastic wrap and refrigerate for at least an hour or up to 3 days before rolling.

If you use cream cheese, amend my instructions for preparing the liquid as follows: In a 2-cup spouted liquid measuring cup, whisk the cream cheese thoroughly with ¼ cup hot (but not boiling) water. There should be absolutely no lumps. Whisk in the lemon juice. Put it in the freezer while you prepare the next steps of the recipe. The idea is to have the liquid at a very cold temperature, not to actually freeze it.

❧ GLUTEN-FREE BUCKWHEAT PIECRUST ❧

Buckwheat has a toasty flavor and a resilient texture that can be your friend or foe. Pancakes: friend. Waffles: foe. A sweet filling will tame its toastiness, making this crust great for gluten-free fruit pies.

Expect a soft and crumbly, not flaky, texture. Because it's gluten-free, you don't need to worry about toughening it by touching it too much. (You might, however, melt the butter if you're too handy.) As with traditional piecrust, refrigerate the dough for a few minutes if it begins to get too soft.

Makes 1 double crust

3 cups buckwheat flour

2 tablespoons sugar

1 teaspoon salt

1 cup (2 sticks) well-chilled unsalted butter or vegetable shortening

Tapioca or rice flour, for rolling out the dough

1. Fill a spouted liquid measuring cup with about 1½ cups of water, plop in some ice cubes, and place it in the freezer while you prepare the next steps of the recipe. The idea is to have more water than you need for the recipe (which will probably use ½ cup or less) at a very cold temperature, not to actually freeze the water or use all 1½ cups in the dough.

2. In a medium bowl, mix the buckwheat, sugar, and salt. Cut ½- to 1-tablespoon-size pieces of butter and drop them into the flour. Toss the fat with the flour to evenly distribute it.

3. Position your hands palms up, fingers loosely curled. Scoop up flour and fat and rub it between your thumb and fingers, letting it fall back into the bowl after rubbing it. Do this, reaching into the bottom and around the sides to incorporate all the flour into the fat, until the mixture resembles coarse sand and the butter is in pea-size pieces, with a few bigger pieces.

4. Take the water out of the freezer. Pour it in a steady thin stream around the bowl for about 5 seconds. Toss to distribute the moisture. If the dough sticks together when you press a bit of it into a ball, it's done. If it doesn't, add more water and toss again. The dough is ready when it is slightly moist and sticks together easily.

5. With firm, brief pressure, gather the dough in 2 roughly equal balls (if one is larger, use that for the bottom crust). Quickly form the dough into thick disks using your palms and thumbs. Wrap the disks individually in plastic wrap. Refrigerate for an hour to 3 days before rolling.

6. Place a sheet of wax or parchment paper on a work surface and dust the paper and your rolling pin with tapioca or rice flour. Remove the plastic wrap from one of the disks and slowly roll out the bottom crust. This dough is much more delicate than gluten-full dough, so don't whack it or rotate it. Simply roll it out, starting each roll at the center and rolling toward the edge, rolling evenly in each direction so the dough forms a large, round shape. Flour your rolling pin as needed to keep the dough from sticking to it.

A NOTE ON ROLLING OUT THE DOUGH: Buckwheat cracks easily, but it also mends easily. The edges of the bottom crust may fall off when you tuck it into the pie plate, but that's okay. Calmly tuck the dough into the plate, then reattach the edges. If the top crust is too delicate to transfer from the counter to the pie, use a medium-size cookie or biscuit cutter to cut liftable shapes from the dough, and place those in patterns on the filling instead of using a traditional top crust.

7. To transfer the dough into the pie plate, place the plate close to the dough but not on the paper, slide your hand under the paper so it cradles the center of the dough, and swiftly flip it into the pan. Flipping dough is sort of like pouring water from a pitcher—if you're tentative about it, you'll make a mess. If you're confident (fake it until you make it), you'll land it in the pan just right, or close enough. Commit to the flip.

continued

8. Once it's in the plate and fairly centered (tug and lift the paper to center the dough, if you need to), peel the wax paper off at a sharp angle. Reattach any edges that fall off and fold them over to form a ridge (if you're making a traditional top crust, wait to form the ridge until the top crust is on the pie). Refrigerate the bottom crust while you assemble the rest of the pie.

9. Roll out the top crust in the same manner as the bottom one. After you've poured the filling into the bottom crust, flip the top crust onto the pie as described above. It will fall apart a bit and create a rustic look. Or you can cut out shapes with a cookie or biscuit cutter and arrange them on top of the filling. A bench scraper is useful for transferring the cutouts from the wax paper to your pie.

10. Bake the pie according to the recipe's instructions. The buckwheat crust will puff up a bit and set just like a wheat-flour crust. Buckwheat's bluish cast makes it harder to tell if the top crust is overbrowning, so keep an eye on it for the last 20 minutes. If the crust starts to get too brown, cover those spots with aluminum foil or a piecrust shield.

❖ GLUTEN-FREE ALMOND FLOUR PIECRUST ❖

Almond flour makes a crumbly, yet dense crust with a light, nutty flavor. It's too delicate to roll out and isn't suitable for top crusts, but it makes a wonderful bottom crust. Save this for cream pies and chiffon pies.

Makes 1 bottom crust

1. In a medium bowl, combine the almond flour, sugar, and salt. Add the butter and stir until the mixture is evenly moist. Add the egg all at once and stir until the mixture is evenly moist. Refrigerate the dough for 15 minutes.

2. Preheat the oven to 350 degrees F.

3. Put the dough into a pie plate and, using your fingers, spread it evenly over the bottom and sides, smoothing the rim. Bake the empty crust for 15 to 20 minutes. The crust is done when it is lightly toasted, slightly puffy, and fragrant. Set it aside to cool on a wire rack before filling.

2 cups almond flour or meal

1 tablespoon sugar

½ teaspoon salt

6 tablespoons butter, melted

1 large egg, beaten

Bob's Red Mill almond flour is available online and at many grocery stores. Almond meal is not almond flour—it is coarser and mixed with almond skins—but it's cheaper and works just fine in this recipe.

❧ ANY-COOKIE-CRUMB CRUST ❧

Sylvester Graham thought cholera was caused by chicken pies, and he advocated a diet of fruit and whole wheat with very sparing use of butter that would ease "bad habits" of the body and mind. The graham cracker is named for him. I doubt very much he intended it to become the inspiration for a nation of sweet piecrusts, but that's, as they say, how the cookie crumbles. This recipe was inspired by *Joy of Cooking*'s crumb crusts.

Makes 1 bottom crust

2 cups crushed cookies

Pinch of salt

½ teaspoon ground cinnamon or ginger (optional)

6 tablespoons butter, melted

Substitute vanilla wafers, chocolate cookies, gingersnaps, or some other crunchy, delicious cookie according to your taste and what might frame the pie filling best.

1. Pulse the cookies in a food processor until they've been smashed to crumbs. If you don't have a food processor, put the cookies in a resealable plastic bag, push the air out of the bag, seal it, and smash the contents with a heavy object. A rolling pin works well. Large cookbooks can do the trick too. Smash until everything is crumbs.

2. In a medium bowl, mix the crumbs with the salt and cinnamon (if using). Pour the melted butter over the cookie crumbs and mix with a fork to combine.

3. Preheat the oven to 350 degrees F.

4. Put the crumb mixture in a 9- to 9½-inch pie plate and, using your fingers, spread it in a thin layer over the bottom and up the sides.

5. Bake the crust for 10 minutes, or until it's slightly fragrant and golden. Cool it on a wire rack before filling. Note: Unlike pastry crusts, you can refrigerate a cookie crust to cool it faster.

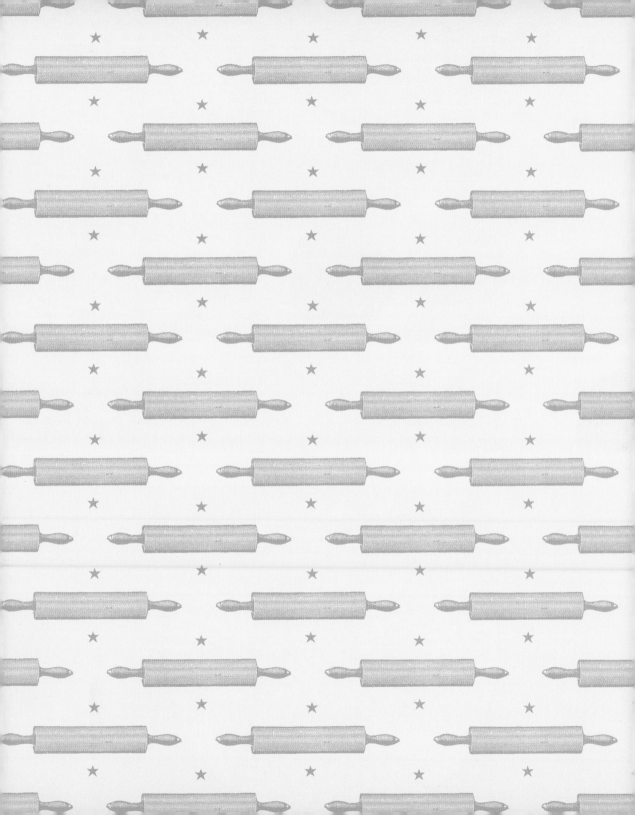

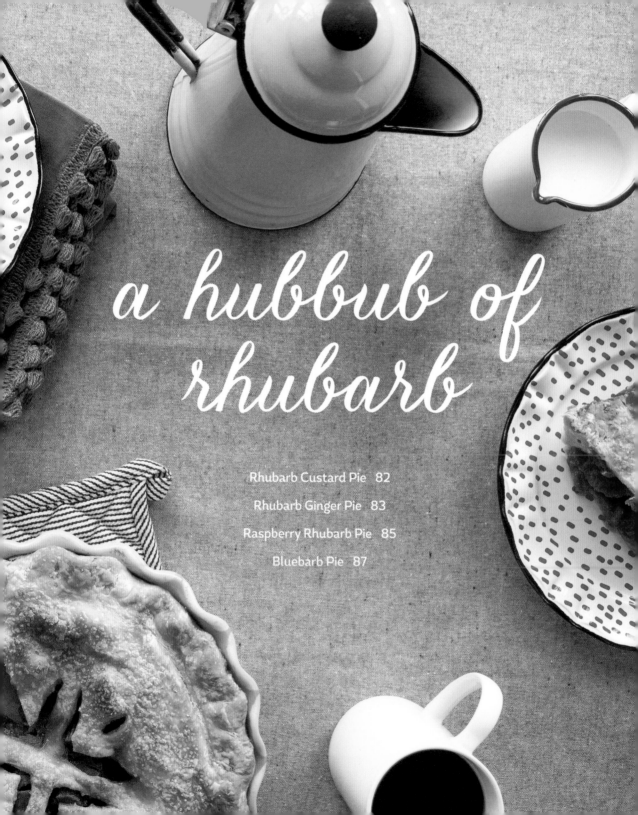

a hubbub of rhubarb

The force that through the green fuse drives the flower
Drives my green age . . .

—DYLAN THOMAS

★　★　★　★　★

Spring announces itself by driving a crown of red stalks through the cold dirt of my new garden. On one end of the plot, a brown foam of mushrooms burbles beneath the cardboard cover I've used to clear the soil of shotweed and dandelion. On the other, two rhubarb plants perk up and check out their new digs. They used to be one rhubarb, a huge crown that led me to believe I had a green thumb and supplied pie to my cold-weather barbecues. It was the first root in my first garden, and the last thing I took when I dissolved my household.

I stood by with a bucket while a friend dug it up, heaved her shovel above the gnarl, and slammed her blade down its middle, cleaving the root in two. Inside, it was a startling soft peach, marbled like orange sherbet, with the firm, bright dryness of a celery root. At my new house, each half got its own three square feet to sleep off the shock of division. While they hunkered under the dirt, I got down to the business of furniture and cupboard arrangement, address changes, and new neighbors. The winter ahead wouldn't last any longer than usual, but I didn't know that then.

In late March, my rhubarb's growth starts with a bubble, its immature petioles a visible pink that bulge until they crack open under Seattle's unreliable sun. Its leaves don't unfurl so much as unfold, accordion-like, into broad green fans

★ ★ ★ ★ ★

that are packed with poisonous oxalic acid and receive rain the way I receive air. Rhubarb plants are tough, irrepressible, needing only a little fertilizer and to be left alone. Most of their care comes directly from the sky. Homegrown rhubarb is as tart as store-bought, but its taste is indescribably more rhubarb-y, which makes its astringency pleasant. A flavor to court rather than combat.

That rhubarb's nickname is "pie plant" should tell you how it's best used, and also why we sugar rhubarb like fruit when it's really a vegetable. When preparing it for pie, make sure to cut off and discard the leaves, and trim the ends where the red color starts. If the stalks are very thick, cut them in half by placing a knife at the middle of a trimmed end and sliding the blade through the stalk. It's an easy, satisfying cut. Some recipes advise peeling the stalks; mine don't. It's an unnecessary step that lessens a rhubarb pie's tart blush.

If you prefer to make your pies with fruit, you probably anticipate rhubarb as much as I do. It appears just as we've forgotten the pleasures of fresh produce and what it's like to be really, truly warm. Rhubarb's arrival kicks off the next half year of better weather and bigger harvests. The fertile seasons when a flower can burst and fade and transform into fruit that glows in the garden like a lit fuse.

⁕ RHUBARB CUSTARD PIE ⁕

I adapted this rhubarb custard pie from an antique Washington State Hothouse Rhubarb Council pamphlet.

This open-faced pie requires less rhubarb than a straight-up rhubarb pie, so it's ideal for that first crop of skinny stalks from the garden.

Makes 1 pie

½ recipe any double-crust pie dough (for a single crust)

3 tablespoons flour

1 cup sugar

½ teaspoon ground nutmeg

Pinch of salt

2 eggs

2 tablespoons whole milk

1 tablespoon unsalted butter, melted

3 cups (about 1 pound) roughly chopped fresh or frozen rhubarb

1. Make the dough and refrigerate it for at least an hour, or overnight. Roll out the bottom crust and place it in a 9-inch pie plate. Tuck the crust into the plate, trim the edges, and fold them into a ridge. Freeze the crust while you prepare the next steps of the recipe.

2. Preheat the oven to 400 degrees F.

3. In a medium bowl, combine the flour, sugar, nutmeg, and salt. In a small bowl, beat the eggs slightly, add the milk, and whisk to combine. Whisk the eggs into the flour mixture. Pour the butter into the flour-egg mixture in a slow stream, whisking as you go. Fold in the rhubarb. Remove the crust from the freezer. Pour the custard into the crust and smooth the surface with a spoon.

4. Bake for 50 to 60 minutes, rotating the pie front to back about halfway through to ensure even baking until the crust is golden and the center remains firm when shaken gently.

5. Cool on a wire rack for at least an hour. Serve warm or at room temperature. Store leftovers in the refrigerator, tightly wrapped, for up to 3 days.

❖ RHUBARB GINGER PIE ❖

This pie was inspired by an English-style jam that Rebecca Staffel's Deluxe Foods used to sell at Seattle farmers' markets. If a flavor combination tastes good as a preserve, it will work well in pie too. I borrowed a jammer's trick to make the filling: macerate the rhubarb and ginger overnight to improve taste and texture. By morning the rhubarb will be soft and sweet, floating in a puddle of its own juice.

Makes 1 pie

1. Combine the rhubarb, granulated sugar, and ginger in a medium bowl, cover it with a dish towel, and let it sit for at least two hours, preferably overnight. The longer you let it sit, the more tender and sweet the rhubarb will be.

2. Make the dough and refrigerate it for at least an hour, or overnight.

3. Add the salt to the rhubarb. Taste and adjust as needed. Stir in the tapioca flour and set the filling aside.

4. Roll out the bottom crust and place it in a 9- to 10-inch pie plate. Tuck the crust into the plate and trim the edges, then refrigerate it while you prepare the next steps of the recipe.

5. Preheat the oven to 425 degrees F.

6. Roll out the top crust and retrieve the bottom crust from the refrigerator.

continued

5 cups (about 2 pounds) fresh or frozen rhubarb sliced ½ inch thick

1¼ cups granulated sugar

2 tablespoons peeled and finely chopped fresh ginger

1 recipe any double-crust pie dough

Pinch of salt

¼ cup tapioca flour

Egg white wash (1 egg white beaten with 1 teaspoon water)

Demerara sugar, for sprinkling

If using frozen rhubarb, defrost it first and drain watery juice away before using in this recipe.

7. Using a slotted spoon, put the rhubarb pieces into the bottom crust. Pour in the juice, stopping about a ½ inch below the rim.

8. Drape the top crust over the filling. Trim, fold, and flute the edges if you like. Cut generous steam vents, brush the crust with the egg white wash, and sprinkle it with the demerara sugar.

9. Bake the pie in the middle of the oven for 15 to 20 minutes, until the crust is blistered and blond. Reduce the heat to 375 degrees F. Bake for 35 to 45 minutes more, until the crust is deeply golden and the juices bubble slowly at the pie's edge. About halfway through, rotate the pie front to back to ensure even baking.

10. Cool on a wire rack for at least an hour. Serve warm or at room temperature. Store leftovers on the kitchen counter loosely wrapped in a towel for up to 3 days.

❖ RASPBERRY RHUBARB PIE ❖

This pie was invented by necessity: I absolutely needed to try the blackcap raspberries I'd found at the Port Townsend Food Co-op, and I couldn't afford to buy enough for a whole pie. Rhubarb to the rescue! It remains one of my all-time favorite pies. You can probably get away with subpar rhubarb in this recipe, but make sure you have fantastic raspberries. Blackcap, golden, ruby red, fresh, or frozen—just make sure they're the kind you can't stop eating. But stop eating them. Unless you want an all-rhubarb pie.

Makes 1 pie

1. Make the dough and refrigerate it for at least an hour, or overnight. Roll out the bottom crust and place it in a 9- to 10-inch pie plate. Tuck the crust into the plate and trim the edges. Refrigerate the crust while you prepare the next steps of the recipe.

2. Preheat the oven to 425 degrees F.

3. In a large bowl, mix the rhubarb with half the raspberries (if fresh; if frozen, use all at once), the granulated sugar, nutmeg, and salt. (Note: Fresh raspberries will smash with a bit of mixing, frozen won't smash as badly.) Taste and adjust the flavors as needed. Stir in the flour and set the filling aside.

4. Roll out the top crust and retrieve the bottom crust from the refrigerator.

continued

1 recipe any double-crust pie dough

2½ cups (about 1 pound) fresh or frozen rhubarb sliced ½ inch thick

2½ cups (about 1 heaping pint) fresh or frozen raspberries

1 cup granulated sugar

Pinch of ground nutmeg

Pinch of salt

5 tablespoons flour

Egg white wash (1 egg white beaten with 1 teaspoon water)

Demerara sugar, for sprinkling

5. Pour the filling into the bottom crust and smooth it into a mound with your hand. (If you're using fresh raspberries, add the remaining ones now.) Drape the top crust over the filling. Trim, fold, and flute the edges if you like. Cut generous steam vents, brush the crust with the egg white wash, and sprinkle it with the demerara sugar.

6. Bake the pie in the middle of the oven for 15 to 20 minutes, until the crust is blond and blistered. Rotate the pie front to back and reduce the heat to 375 degrees F. Bake for 35 to 45 minutes more, until the crust is golden brown and the juices are thickened and bubble slowly through the vents.

7. Cool on a wire rack for at least an hour. Serve warm or at room temperature. Store leftovers on the kitchen counter loosely wrapped in a towel for up to 3 days.

❖ BLUEBARB PIE ❖

Strawberry rhubarb pie is iconic in a particularly maternal way. On multiple occasions I've been told by complete strangers not to mess with it because "if you mess with strawberry rhubarb pie, you mess with Mom." I asked the most recent repeater of this quote, "By 'mess,' do you mean change the recipe, bake it badly, or make an actual mess with it?" He said, "I mean don't mess with Mom." Fair enough.

Instead I'll offer a demure combination that deserves a little limelight: blueberry rhubarb pie, or "bluebarb" pie for short. Blueberries are milder and deeper-tasting, less acidic and sweet than strawberries, and will stain your bib just as badly. If this pie isn't sweet enough for dessert that just means it's perfect for breakfast. And if you really want a strawberry rhubarb pie, you can use this recipe to make one. Just substitute strawberries for the blueberries.

Makes 1 pie

1. Make the dough and refrigerate it for at least an hour, or overnight. Roll out the bottom crust and place it in a 9- to 10-inch pie plate. Tuck the crust into the plate and trim the edges. Refrigerate the crust while you prepare the next steps of the recipe.

2. Preheat the oven to 425 degrees F.

3. In a large bowl, mix the rhubarb with the blueberries, granulated sugar, lemon juice, nutmeg, and salt. Taste and adjust the flavors as needed. Stir in the flour and butter and set the filling aside.

4. Roll out the top crust and retrieve the bottom crust from the refrigerator.

continued

1 recipe any double-crust pie dough

2½ cups (about 1 pound) fresh or frozen rhubarb sliced ½ inch thick

2½ cups (1 heaping pint) fresh or frozen blueberries

1 cup granulated sugar

Juice of ½ medium lemon (about 1½ tablespoons)

Pinch of ground nutmeg

Pinch of salt

5 tablespoons flour

2 tablespoons chilled unsalted butter, cut into small chunks

Egg white wash (1 egg white beaten with 1 teaspoon water)

Demerara sugar, for sprinkling

5. Pour the filling into the bottom crust, mound it with your hands, and drape the top crust over it. Trim, fold, and flute the edges if you like. Cut generous steam vents, brush the top crust with the egg white wash, and sprinkle it with the demerara sugar.

6. Bake the pie in the middle of the oven for 15 to 20 minutes, or until the crust is blond and blistered. Rotate the pie front to back and reduce the heat to 375 degrees F. Bake about 35 to 45 minutes more, until the crust is golden brown and the juices are thickened and bubble slowly through the vents.

7. Cool on a wire rack for at least an hour. Serve warm or at room temperature. Store leftovers on the kitchen counter loosely wrapped in a towel for up to 3 days.

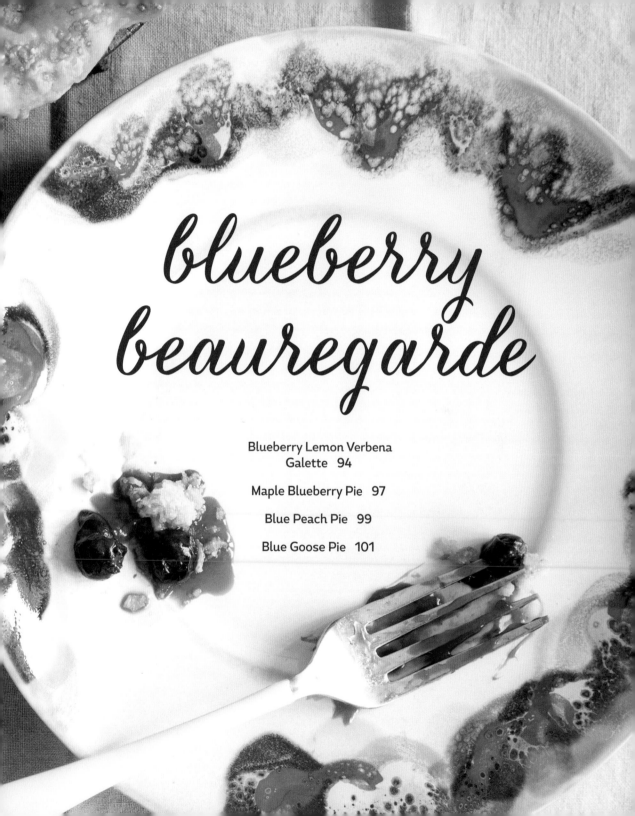

blueberry beauregarde

Blueberry Lemon Verbena
Galette   94

Maple Blueberry Pie   97

Blue Peach Pie   99

Blue Goose Pie   101

*I have finally discovered the color of
the atmosphere. It is violet.*

—CLAUDE MONET

★　★　★　★　★

Blue doesn't occur naturally in fruit, so when we call a blueberry blue, really we mean that it's like blue, or we wish it were blue, or it's blue the way hazel eyes are sometimes green.

Blueberry's skin gives blueberry its (mis)name: it's not blue but violet, sometimes burnished with silver. When Roald Dahl named the obnoxious Violet Beauregarde in *Charlie and the Chocolate Factory*, he prefigured her transformation into a giant blueberry with a more accurate name than the berry itself can boast. When her father screams, "Violet! You're turning violet!" he's calling out a metaphor for mis-ripening, a spoiled child showing her spoilage by blowing up into the literal meaning of her name. The metamorphosis shows Violet's "true colors" by showing their consequence, but it also tames her wildly chattering mouth and grabby hands. Blueberry Violet is so mild she must be pushed offstage.

So it's not just violet-ness that Violet has in common with blueberries; it's her sudden surprising mildness. When perfectly ripe, blueberries are neither too

★　★　★　★　★

tart nor too sweet, as easy to eat raw as they are to bake. They can fit themselves into just about any fruit combination or baked good; alone, they impress with their steadiness, not their dazzle. They're like the note taker in the group project, recording louder fruits' flights of fancy and bringing them down to earth long enough to make something actually happen, so it's not just pie in the sky.

I should mention I'm talking about highbush or rabbiteye blueberries, which grow well in the Pacific Northwest and elsewhere, not the shrubby lowbush varieties of the Northeast, which are smaller and stronger tasting than their cousins and often called "wild blueberry." Both work equally well in any recipes calling for blueberries. Use whichever you can find.

Homegrown blueberries have a piney bite that's hard to find at the store and can even be elusive at farmers' markets. If available blueberries fall short, forgive them. They'll taste better after they've been baked. Blueberries can be, like Violet Beauregarde, much improved by radical transformation.

❖ BLUEBERRY LEMON VERBENA GALETTE ❖

Blue and yellow have an affinity for each other, each primary hue smug in its irreducibility on the color wheel. When they appear together in a Cub Scout uniform or on the Swedish flag, for example, the effect is one of solid, capable brightness, like the smile of a real estate agent you can actually trust. Blueberry and lemon are a cheerful pair for similar reasons, but their relationship is more symbiotic—mild blueberries benefit from lemon's acidic kick, and lemon's sharp sweetness can be softened into easy palatability with a handful of blueberries.

This galette owes its invention to that classic fruit pairing, and to a lemon verbena plant I adopted one summer. The result is a blueberry-lemon flavor with a trace of floral herbiness—the sort of pie that seems familiar and strange at the same time.

Makes 1 galette

1 recipe Galette Dough (page 70)

4 cups (2 pints) fresh or frozen blueberries

½ cup granulated sugar

Juice of 1 medium lemon (2 to 3 tablespoons)

Pinch of salt

10 lemon verbena leaves, finely chopped (optional)

5 tablespoons flour

2 tablespoons chilled unsalted butter, cut into small chunks

Egg white wash (1 egg white beaten with 1 teaspoon water) or heavy cream

Demerara sugar, for sprinkling

1. Make the dough. Let it rest in the refrigerator for an hour while you prepare the next steps of the recipe.

2. Preheat the oven to 450 degrees F.

3. In a large bowl, mix the blueberries, granulated sugar, lemon juice, salt, and lemon verbena. Taste and adjust salt and sweet as necessary. Add the flour and butter and stir to combine. Set the filling aside.

4. Retrieve the dough from the refrigerator. On a floured surface, roll it out into about an ⅛-inch-thick round. It will be large—14 inches, maybe bigger. (The dough doesn't need to be perfectly round, but it lays better in the pan if it is roundish.)

continued

Trim the edges or patch the dough as needed to make it more round. Fold the dough into fourths, transfer it to the pan, and unfold it, tucking the dough gently into the edges of the pan. Let the excess drape over the edge of the pan.

5. Pour the filling into the dough. Grab some of the excess dough and pull it toward the center of the galette. Grab another spot about three or four inches down and pull it toward the center, continuing until you have used all the dough to create a soft ruffle of crust surrounding a juicy blue center. Brush the dough with the egg white wash, and sprinkle it with the demerara sugar.

6. Bake the galette in the middle of the oven for 10 to 15 minutes, until the crust is blistered and blond. Reduce the heat to 350 degrees F. Bake for 40 to 50 minutes more, until the crust is deeply golden and the juices bubble slowly at the galette's edge.

7. Cool on a wire rack for at least an hour. Serve warm or at room temperature. Store leftovers on the kitchen counter loosely wrapped in a towel for up to 3 days.

❖ MAPLE BLUEBERRY PIE ❖

This pie contains all the flavors of the morning except for bacon, which you could serve on the side, I suppose, if you wanted to call this breakfast. Maple syrup's sweet warmth frames the berries' mild, unflashy flavor in a filling that tastes just sweet enough, just spiced enough—pleased with itself but not full of itself. It is just what it is: the finest blueberries in the finest maple syrup wrapped in pastry instead of pancakes, welcome at any meal of the day.

Makes 1 pie

1. Make the dough and refrigerate it for at least an hour, or up to 3 days. Roll out the bottom crust and place it in a 9- to 10-inch pie plate. Tuck the crust into the plate and trim the edges. Refrigerate the crust while you prepare the next steps of the recipe.

2. Preheat the oven to 425 degrees F.

3. In a large bowl, mix the blueberries, maple syrup, lemon juice, cinnamon, and salt. Taste and adjust the syrup, lemon, spice or salt as necessary. Add flour and butter and stir to combine. Set the filling aside.

4. Roll out the top crust and retrieve the bottom crust from the refrigerator.

continued

1 recipe any double-crust pie dough

5 cups (not quite 2 pounds) fresh or frozen blueberries

½ cup high-quality maple syrup

Juice of ½ medium lemon (about 1½ tablespoons)

½ teaspoon ground cinnamon

Pinch of salt

5 tablespoons flour

2 tablespoons chilled unsalted butter, cut into small chunks

Egg white wash (1 egg white beaten with 1 teaspoon water)

Demerara sugar, for sprinkling

Use high-quality maple syrup. There's no point in using fake maple syrup—you might as well use corn syrup if you're going to go that route.

5. Pour the filling into the bottom crust, dot with butter, and drape the top crust over it. Trim, fold, and flute the edges if you like. Cut generous steam vents, brush the crust with the egg white wash, and sprinkle it with the demerara sugar.

6. Bake the pie in the middle of the oven for 15 to 20 minutes, until the crust is blistered and blond. Reduce the heat to 375 degrees F. Bake for 35 to 45 minutes more, until the crust is deeply golden and the juices bubble slowly at the pie's edge. Rotate the pie front to back halfway through to ensure even baking.

7. Cool on a wire rack for at least an hour. Serve warm or at room temperature. Store leftovers on the kitchen counter loosely wrapped in a towel for up to 3 days.

❖ BLUE PEACH PIE ❖

Once again, blueberries bring out the best in another fruit; this time they provide a steadying influence. Peaches are flashy and sexy, gorgeous and tempting on their own. Every time I throw a summer pie party, guests snatch up the peach pie faster than you can say "ice cream." When speckled with a couple cups of blueberries, peaches tone down their siren song just long enough to show you what else they're capable of, how many tunes they can sing besides "summer."

Make this pie with a lattice crust. Orange and blue fight a bit in the eye, which makes them hotter, deeper, and brighter, not so stereotypically sweet. Your eyes will recognize the tone of this pie before the first forkful meets your mouth.

Makes 1 pie

1. Make the dough. Roll out the bottom crust and place it in a 9- or 10-inch pie plate. Tuck the crust into the plate and trim the edges. Refrigerate the crust while you prepare the next steps of the recipe.

2. Preheat the oven to 425 degrees F.

3. In a large bowl, gently combine the blueberries, peaches, granulated sugar, brown sugar, salt, nutmeg, and lemon juice. Taste and adjust the flavors as needed. Gently stir in the flour and set the filling aside.

4. Roll out the top crust and retrieve the bottom crust from the refrigerator.

continued

1 recipe any double-crust pie dough

2 cups (1 pint) fresh or frozen blueberries

3 cups (about 1 pound) unpeeled peaches sliced ¼ inch thick and pitted

½ cup granulated sugar

¼ cup (packed) brown sugar

Pinch of salt

Big pinch of ground nutmeg

Juice of ½ medium lemon (about 1½ tablespoons)

⅓ cup flour

2 tablespoons chilled unsalted butter, cut into small pieces

Egg white wash (1 egg white beaten with 1 teaspoon water)

Demerara sugar, for sprinkling

Flour is a more dependable thickener for irrepressibly juicy peaches. Brown sugar mixed with white sugar lends a slight caramel flavor, and a little lemon binds it all together.

5. Pour the filling into the bottom crust, dot it with the butter, and drape the top crust over it. Trim, fold, and flute the edges if you like. Cut generous steam vents, brush the crust with the egg white wash, and sprinkle it with the demerara sugar.

6. Bake the pie in the middle of the oven for 15 to 20 minutes, until the crust is blistered and blond. Reduce the heat to 375 degrees F. Bake for another 35 to 45 minutes more, until the crust is deeply golden and the juices bubble slowly at the pie's edge. Rotate the pie front to back halfway through to ensure even baking.

7. Cool on a wire rack for at least an hour. Serve warm or at room temperature. Store leftovers on the kitchen counter loosely wrapped in a towel for up to 3 days.

⚓ BLUE GOOSE PIE ⚓

This is a pie of two minds. One is sweet, the other tart, and they don't always agree. That's it's charm, in my book—a single bite contains multitudes. Gooseberries are traditionally paired in Victorian recipes with elderflowers, so a little St. Germain can be a fun addition. Honey frames the gooseberries' tart, flowery taste while white sugar perks up the blueberries. Use green or purple gooseberries. Or both. In the Pacific Northwest they're available for just a short while in July. If you see some, snatch them up. They have no substitute.

Makes 1 pie

1. Make the dough. Roll out the bottom crust and place it in a 9- or 10-inch pie plate. Tuck the crust into the plate and trim the edges. Refrigerate the crust while you prepare the next steps of the recipe.

2. Preheat the oven to 425 degrees F.

3. In a large bowl, crush ½ cup of the gooseberries and ½ cup of the blueberries. Add the rest of the fruit whole, then the honey, sugar, salt, and St. Germain, and gently combine. Taste and adjust the flavors as needed. Gently stir in the tapioca flour and set the filling aside.

4. Roll out the top crust and retrieve the bottom crust from the refrigerator.

continued

1 recipe any double-crust pie dough

2 cups (1 pint) fresh gooseberries (green or purple)

2 cups (1 pint) fresh or frozen blueberries

½ cup honey

⅓ heaping cup sugar

Pinch of salt

2 tablespoons St. Germain (optional)

5 tablespoons tapioca flour

Egg white wash (1 egg white beaten with 1 teaspoon water)

Demerara sugar, for sprinkling

5. Pour the filling into the bottom crust and drape the top crust over it. Trim, fold, and flute the edges if you like. Cut generous steam vents, brush the crust with the egg white wash, and sprinkle it with the demerara sugar.

6. Bake the pie in the middle of the oven for 15 to 20 minutes, until the crust is blistered and blond. Reduce the heat to 375 degrees F. Bake for another 35 to 45 minutes more, until the crust is deeply golden and the juices bubble slowly at the pie's edge. Rotate the pie halfway through to ensure even baking.

7. Cool on a wire rack for at least an hour. Serve warm or at room temperature. Store leftovers on the kitchen counter loosely wrapped in a towel for up to 3 days.

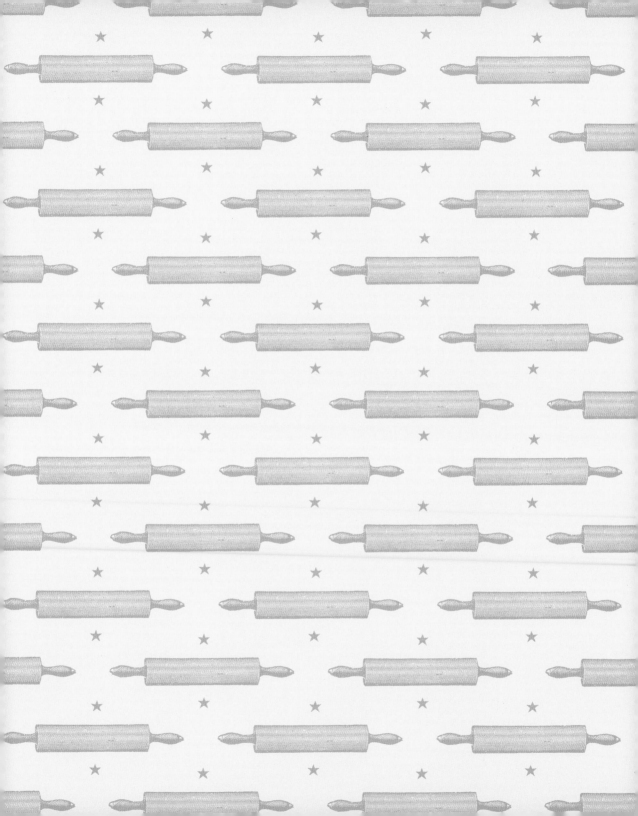

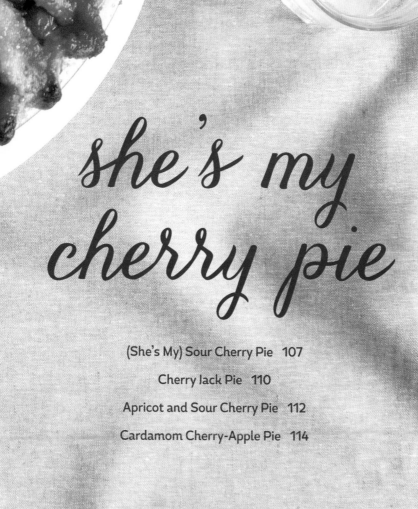

she's my cherry pie

She's my cherry pie . . . tastes so good
makes a grown man cry.

—"CHERRY PIE," WARRANT (1990)

★   ★   ★   ★   ★

"Cherry Pie" had a short season. Warrant sang their hair-metal hit the year before Nirvana exploded the charts with raw fury and catchy hooks, making cock rock look postured and passé in comparison. The song remains preserved in the binders of karaoke hosts across the nation, larger in memory than it was during its day.

Fresh cherry pie has an even shorter—but sweeter—season. Once I lived next door to an overgrown pie-cherry tree. It fruit-bombed the back patio and drove the birds nuts, which drove my cat nuts, which made me an extra-motivated cherry picker. Our neighbor wasn't interested in the fruit or the cleanup job, so I'd pull branches over to my side and pick as many as I could reach, balancing precariously on deck furniture and tall chairs. If the summer was a good one, cherries reddened the week following Independence Day. If I happened to be out of town that week, I'd come home to pecked away, sun-shriveled fruit, spoiled barely a week after ripening.

Lucky for me, my parents pack thirty pounds of sour and sweet cherries into their freezer each summer. When I come home to visit, I'll find a bag of cherries defrosting on the kitchen counter, a not-so-subtle sign that there is an afternoon of cherry pie-making in my near future.

Sour and tart cherries are also called pie cherries. I'm talking about Montmorency, Morello, or Balaton, not bing, Lapin, or Rainier. Sour cherries are a hybrid of sweet cherries and astringent, cold-hardy ground cherries, with higher acidity, less sugar, and more delicate fruit. Baked, they're hard to beat. Sweet cherries are juice- and sugar-packed, perfect fresh, ruined by extra sweeteners, decimated by an oven. Try sweet cherries in unbaked chiffon pies like Black Cherry Chiffon Pie with Chocolate Cookie Crust (page 209), which will put them under the spotlight they deserve without withering them with heat.

⁂ (SHE'S MY) SOUR CHERRY PIE ⁂

Warrant's pop innuendo was soundly sourced. Cherry pie is sweet and tart, juicy and sexy, fresh at July Fourth when we've just worn in our new pairs of short-shorts. I can't think of cherry pie without also thinking of bare legs, sweet peas, soft hot breezes, and getting swatted by branches while picking sun-warmed fruit.

You can turn this into a galette by using the Galette Dough (page 70), following all other instructions as is.

Makes 1 pie

1. Make the dough and refrigerate it for at least an hour, or overnight. Roll out the bottom crust and place it in a 9- or 10-inch pie plate. Tuck the crust into the plate and trim the edges. Refrigerate the crust while you prepare the next steps of the recipe.

2. In a large bowl, combine the cherries with the granulated sugar, lemon juice, almond extract, salt, and nutmeg. Taste and adjust the flavors as needed. Stir in the flour and butter and set the filling aside.

3. Preheat the oven to 425 degrees F.

4. Roll out the top crust and cut into strips for a lattice (if you wish). Retrieve the bottom crust from the refrigerator.

continued

1 recipe any double-crust pie dough

5 cups (about 2 pounds) pitted, fresh or frozen, sour or tart (but not sweet) cherries

1 cup granulated sugar

1 teaspoon freshly squeezed lemon juice

½ teaspoon almond extract

Pinch of salt

Pinch of ground nutmeg

5 tablespoons flour

2 tablespoons chilled unsalted butter, cut into small chunks

Egg white wash (1 egg white beaten with 1 teaspoon water)

Demerara sugar, for sprinkling

Most of the nation's pie cherry supply comes from Michigan, but they're also grown in the Northeast and Northwest. They have a short season, spoil easily, and, like Gravenstein apples, have a devoted following. As a result, pie cherries can be quite dear at the check stand. Frozen or fresh, they're worth every penny.

5. Pour the filling into the bottom crust, mound it with your hands, and drape the top crust over it. Trim, fold, and flute the edges if you like (see "How to Weave a Classic Lattice," page 50). Cut generous steam vents (if you're not making a lattice), brush the crust with the egg white wash, and sprinkle it with the demerara sugar.

6. Bake the pie in the middle of the oven for 15 to 20 minutes, until the crust looks blistered and blond. Reduce the heat to 375 degrees F. Bake for another 35 to 45 minutes more, rotating the pie front to back about halfway through to ensure even baking, until the crust is deeply golden and the juices are thickened and bubble slowly through the vents.

7. Cool the pie completely before serving, at least a few hours. Store leftovers on the kitchen counter loosely wrapped in a towel for up to 3 days.

❧ CHERRY JACK PIE ❧

This pie reminds me of the last sip of an Old-Fashioned cocktail, when the glass is warm and smells like whiskey, and you can finally reach the cherry garnish. I like using Jack Daniels whiskey for this one—there's something about that mid-shelf, sour-mash taste that suits sour cherries. Montmorency cherries, if you can get them, are best for this pie. If you use frozen cherries, smash some of them up a bit with a spoon before piling them into the crust. They'll collapse around the whole cherries and prop them up.

Makes 1 pie

1 recipe any double-crust pie dough

5 cups (about 2 pounds) fresh or frozen sour cherries

1 cup granulated sugar

3 tablespoons Jack Daniels whiskey

½ teaspoon vanilla extract

Dash of cocktail bitters (optional)

Pinch of ground nutmeg

Pinch of salt

5 tablespoons flour

2 tablespoons chilled unsalted butter, cut into chunks

Egg white wash (1 egg white beaten with 1 teaspoon water)

Demerara sugar, for sprinkling

1. Make the dough and refrigerate it for at least an hour, or overnight. Roll out the bottom crust and place it in a 9- or 10-inch pie plate. Tuck the crust into the plate and trim the edges. Refrigerate the crust while you prepare the next steps of the recipe.

2. In a large bowl, combine the cherries with the granulated sugar, whiskey, vanilla, bitters (if using), nutmeg, and salt. Taste and adjust the flavors as needed. Stir in the flour and butter and set the filling aside.

3. Preheat the oven to 425 degrees F.

4. Roll out the top crust and cut into strips for a lattice (if you wish). Retrieve the bottom crust from the refrigerator.

5. Pour the filling into the bottom crust, mound it with your hands, and drape the top crust over it. Trim, fold, and flute the edges if you like (see "How to Weave a Classic Lattice," page 50). Cut generous steam vents (if you're not making a lattice), brush the crust with the egg white wash, and sprinkle it with the demerara sugar.

6. Bake the pie in the middle of the oven for 15 to 20 minutes, until the crust looks dry, blistered, and blond. Reduce the heat to 375 degrees F. Bake for another 35 to 45 minutes more, rotating the pie front to back about halfway through to ensure even baking, until the crust is deeply golden and the juices are thickened and bubble slowly through the vents.

7. Cool the pie completely before serving, at least a few hours. Store leftovers on the kitchen counter loosely wrapped in a towel for up to 3 days.

Top with a lattice crust, if you like, or turn this into a galette by using the Galette Dough (page 70), following all other instructions as is.

❖ APRICOT AND SOUR CHERRY PIE ❖

There's something adult about apricots, regardless of their prevalence in baby food. In comparison to sweet plums and pluots, which ripen around the same time, apricots are self-contained, confident. Their downy pale-peach skin isn't as flashy as the shine of plum purple, and their juices aren't quite as outgoing. Apricots don't need special effects to get our attention; they already have it.

In this pie, inspired by *Bubby's Homemade Pies*, thick wedges of golden apricot curl around lipstick-red sour cherries. Brown sugar adds a caramel sweetness to both. If your apricots are swoon-worthy, don't gussy them up with almond extract. They'll be perfect just as they are.

Makes 1 pie

1 recipe any double-crust pie dough

2½ cups (about 1 pound) fresh or frozen pitted sour cherries

2½ cups (about 1 pound) apricots, halved or quartered depending on size and pitted

1 cup (packed) light brown sugar

Juice of ½ medium lemon (about 1½ tablespoons)

½ teaspoon almond extract (optional)

Big pinch of salt

Pinch of ground nutmeg

4 tablespoons flour

2 tablespoons chilled unsalted butter, cut into chunks

Egg white wash (1 egg white beaten with 1 teaspoon water)

Demerara sugar, for sprinkling

1. Make the dough and refrigerate it for at least an hour, or overnight. Roll out the bottom crust and place it in a 9- or 10-inch pie plate. Tuck the crust into the plate and trim the edges. Refrigerate the crust while you prepare the next steps of the recipe.

2. In a medium bowl, gently combine the cherries, apricots, brown sugar, lemon juice, almond extract (if using), salt, and nutmeg. Taste and adjust the flavors as needed. Gently stir in the flour and butter and set the filling aside.

3. Preheat the oven to 425 degrees F.

4. Roll out the top crust and cut into strips for a lattice (if you wish). Retrieve the bottom crust from the refrigerator.

5. Pour the filling into the bottom crust, mound it with your hands, and drape the top crust over it. Trim, fold, and flute the edges if you like (see "How to Weave a Classic Lattice," page 50). Cut generous steam vents (if you're not making a lattice), brush the crust with the egg white wash, and sprinkle it with the demerara sugar.

6. Bake the pie in the middle of the oven for 15 to 20 minutes, until the crust looks dry, blistered, and blond. Reduce the heat to 375 degrees F. Bake for another 35 to 45 minutes more, rotating the pie front to back about halfway through to ensure even baking, until the crust is deeply golden and the juices are thickened and bubble slowly through the vents.

7. Cool the pie completely before serving, at least a few hours. Store leftovers on the kitchen counter loosely wrapped in a towel for up to 3 days.

❧ CARDAMOM CHERRY-APPLE PIE ❧

The strongest flavors of this pie are concentrated in the cherries, which are macerated overnight in brandy, sugar, and cardamom, then laced into a plain apple filling that frames their strong spice. Each bite is an exercise in contrasts: sweetened cherries to tart apples, warm boozy spices to barely enhanced fruit.

Fresh apples during cherry season are suspect, but not frozen cherries during apple season. Make this pie with frozen sour cherries in August or September, when the first pie apples appear. Gravenstein, Akane, or Cortland are my favorites.

Makes 1 pie

1½ cups (about 1 pound) fresh or frozen, pitted sour cherries

¾ cup granulated sugar, divided

½ cup brandy

¼ teaspoon ground cardamom

1 recipe any double-crust pie dough

3 unpeeled, tart pie apples, sliced ⅛ inch thick and cored (about 4 cups)

1 medium almost-ripe Bartlett pear, sliced ⅛ inch thick and cored

Juice of ½ medium lemon (about 1 tablespoon)

Pinch of salt

Pinch of ground nutmeg

4 tablespoons flour

1. Combine the cherries, ½ cup of the granulated sugar, brandy, and cardamom in a medium bowl, cover it with a dish towel, and let it sit for at least two hours, preferably overnight. The longer you let them sit, the more remarkable they'll taste.

2. Make the dough and refrigerate it for at least an hour, or overnight. Roll out the bottom crust and place it in a 9- or 10-inch pie plate. Tuck the crust into the plate and trim the edges. Refrigerate the crust while you prepare the next steps of the recipe.

3. Preheat the oven to 425 degrees F.

4. In a medium bowl, combine the apples and pear with the remaining ¼ cup granulated sugar, lemon juice, salt, nutmeg, and flour. Stir in the macerated cherries and set the filling aside.

5. Roll out the top crust or cut into strips for a lattice, and retrieve the bottom crust from the refrigerator.

6. Pour the filling into the bottom crust, mound it with your hands, and dot it with the butter. Drape the top crust over it. Trim, fold, and flute the edges if you like (see "How to Weave a Classic Lattice," page 50). Cut generous steam vents (if you're not making a lattice), brush the crust with the egg white wash, and sprinkle it with the demerara sugar.

7. Bake the pie in the middle of the oven for 15 to 20 minutes, until the crust looks blistered and blond. Reduce the heat to 375 degrees F. Bake for another 35 to 45 minutes more, rotating the pie front to back about halfway through to ensure even baking, until the crust is deeply golden and the juices are thickened and bubble slowly through the vents.

8. Cool the pie on a wire rack for at least an hour before serving. Serve warm or at room temperature. Store leftovers on the kitchen counter loosely wrapped in a towel for up to 3 days.

2 tablespoons butter

Egg white wash (1 egg white beaten with 1 teaspoon water)

Demerara sugar, for sprinkling

the perfect peach

O, to take what we love inside,

to carry within us an orchard . . .

—"FROM BLOSSOMS," LI-YOUNG LEE

★ ★ ★ ★ ★

The best peaches arrive at farmers' markets in late July and early August, blushed and fuzzed, so fat with juice and easily bruised it's too sweet a risk not to touch them. Their appearance is preceded by a parade of summer fruit: strawberries first, then apricots and plums. Raspberries, then cherries. And then, right before blackberries, a month before apples: peaches. Pie season in full swing.

Which means the season is half over. That's when a particular kind of midsummer anxiety hits me. A buzzy cocktail of pleasure and greed, with a little existential dread and the insouciance of being garden-fed for months now: how to cook with it all, eat it all? Impossible! Wanting it all, I'll fail before I begin.

So starts my annual hunt for one perfect peach.

How many times have I patiently ripened a handsome bag of peaches on the counter, only to find their soft weight was a lie of tasteless mush? To prevent nasty surprises, smell the peaches, don't squeeze them. If they smell like the blush of their skins—honey, a little rose, indelible peach—they're ready. This is a hard test to do at the supermarket, where peaches need their bright unripeness to survive the shipping process. They'll smell like nothing much. A gamble at best.

When I see peaches displayed in soft paper crating, I take it as a sure sign of quality and make a beeline for the biggest one. Why else would the grower go to the trouble and expense of protecting peaches from themselves? Buy those, take them carefully home, don't doctor them with sugar or heat. Eat the

* * * * *

peach fresh. Reserve almost-perfect peaches for pie; save ball-of-sand peaches for the garbage bin.

"Few fruits are quite so reliant on 'the moment,'" writes Nigel Slater. Peach pie, too, is a trick of timing. Unripe peaches aren't much improved by baking. Frozen peaches are enormously juicy and often mushy, their delicate cells blown out and leaking, able to suggest the sweetness of high summer but not its velvet texture. You're likely to make peach pie in the heat of an August kitchen, each muggy second melting the dough to your countertop. Stay cool by chilling the dough whenever it gets too soft, and don't let juicy peaches come in contact with pie dough until the absolute last second possible before putting them in the oven. Some recipes suggest scattering the bottom crust with a little cornmeal to soak up juices, but I've never liked the grit it adds. A better idea would be to bake at night or in the morning, before the temper of midday.

Speaking of juice, peaches are extremely low in pectin and require a firm dose of thickener to help them set up in pie. This is especially true for any peach pie recipes that are sweetened with honey or maple syrup.

Nectarines are peaches with a recessive gene for baldness. Use them instead of peaches in any recipe. Their smooth skins are more dependably toothsome, which saves you the time of peeling fruit. I don't peel peaches, either, unless their skin is too fuzzy to adore. Either fruit, with skins or without, helps "carry within us an orchard" for the rest of the year.

❖ PEACH POTPIE ❖

The only difference between a peach potpie and a peach pie is a bottom crust: peach pie has one, peach potpie doesn't.

Need to bake a pie two or three days before anyone can enjoy it? Make a peach potpie. Peaches are notoriously, deliriously juicy. Given a few days to sulk on the counter, they'll sog up a bottom crust like no one's business. If you can eat the pie right away, I'd recommend a traditional double-crust pie. There's just no beating that.

Makes 1 pie

1. Make the dough and refrigerate it for at least an hour, or overnight.

2. If the peaches are very fuzzy, skin them before slicing. The easiest way is to dip them in boiling water for 10 seconds and then shock them in an ice bath. The peels will shred from the fruit with just a little rubbing. If the peaches have toothsome skins, leave them on. Slice them ¼ inch thick and put them in a medium bowl. Add the honey, salt, nutmeg, and lemon juice. Taste and adjust the flavors as needed. Gently stir in the flour and set the filling aside.

3. Preheat the oven to 425 degrees F.

4. Using a slotted spoon, put the peaches in a medium cast-iron pan. Pour in the juice, stopping about a ½ inch below the rim. Dot the filling with the butter.

5. Roll out the top crust and drape it over the filling. Trim it and crimp or flute the edges.

continued

½ recipe any double-crust pie dough (for a single crust)

5 large or 6 medium ripe peaches or nectarines (about 2 pounds)

½ cup floral-tasting honey

⅛ teaspoon salt

⅛ teaspoon ground nutmeg

Juice of ½ medium lemon (about 1½ tablespoons)

5 to 6 tablespoons flour (depending on how juicy the peaches are)

2 tablespoons chilled unsalted butter, cut into small pieces

Egg white wash (1 egg white beaten with 1 teaspoon water)

Demerara sugar, for sprinkling

Peach potpie can be very messy while baking because the crust doesn't contain the juices as firmly as a double-crust would. Compensate by baking the pie on a rimmed baking sheet to catch drips.

6. Cut generous steam vents, brush the crust with the egg white wash, and sprinkle it with the demerara sugar.

7. Bake the pie in the middle of the oven for 15 to 20 minutes, or until the crust looks dry, blistered, and blond. Reduce the heat to 375 degrees F. Bake for another 35 to 45 minutes more, rotating the pie front to back about halfway through to ensure even baking, until the crust is deeply golden and the juices are thickened and bubble slowly through the vents.

8. Cool the pie completely before serving, at least a few hours. Store leftovers on the kitchen counter loosely wrapped in a towel for up to 3 days.

❖ PEACH WHISKEY PIE ❖

Sweet peaches laced with booze and soaked in honey. You're probably already thinking what I'm about to say: if cherry pie is a virgin's euphemism, peach whiskey pie is Mary Magdalene's bawdy joke. Each bite is like a long talk on a summer porch, crackling with sugar, spinning with alcohol. An easy satisfaction that's all the more interesting when enjoyed without a shadow of regret.

Makes 1 pie

1. Make the dough and refrigerate it for at least an hour, or overnight. Roll out the bottom crust and place it in a 9- to 10-inch pie plate. Tuck the crust into the plate and trim the edges. Refrigerate the crust while you prepare the next steps of the recipe.

2. If the peaches are very fuzzy, skin them before slicing. The easiest way is to dip them in boiling water for 10 seconds and then shock them in an ice bath. The peels will shred from the fruit with just a little rubbing. If the peaches have toothsome skins, leave them on. Slice them ¼ inch thick and put them in a medium bowl. Add the honey, sugar, lemon juice, whiskey, nutmeg, and salt. Taste and adjust the flavors as needed. Gently stir in the flour and set the filling aside.

3. Roll out the top crust and retrieve the bottom crust from the refrigerator.

4. Using a slotted spoon, put the peaches into the bottom crust. Pour in the juice, stopping about a ½ inch below the rim. Dot the filling with the butter, drape the top crust over it, trim the edges, and crimp or flute them.

continued

1 recipe any double crust pie dough

5 to 6 large ripe peaches or nectarines (about 2 pounds)

½ cup floral-tasting honey

¼ cup sugar

Juice of ½ medium lemon (about 1½ tablespoons)

2 to 3 tablespoons bourbon or rye whiskey

⅛ teaspoon ground nutmeg

Pinch of salt

5 to 6 tablespoons flour (depending on how juicy the peaches are)

2 tablespoons chilled unsalted butter, cut into small pieces

Egg white wash (1 egg white beaten with 1 teaspoon water)

Demerara sugar, for sprinkling

5. Preheat the oven to 425 degrees F and freeze the pie while you wait for the oven to heat up.

6. Right before baking, cut generous steam vents, brush the crust with the egg white wash, and sprinkle it with the demerara sugar.

7. Bake the pie in the middle of the oven for 15 to 20 minutes, or until the crust looks dry, blistered, and blond. Reduce the heat to 375 degrees F and bake for at least 35 to 45 minutes more, rotating the pie front to back about halfway through to ensure even baking, until the crust is deeply golden and the juices are thickened and bubble slowly through the vents.

8. Cool the pie completely before serving, at least a few hours. Store leftovers on the kitchen counter loosely wrapped in a towel for up to 3 days.

❖ PEACH GINGER PIE ❖

This is my prize-winning pie, made originally with the Purple-Ribbon Piecrust (page 66). A pinch of cayenne adds a flicker of heat. Honey softens ginger's potentially overpowering punch. And peaches, well . . . peaches are peaches. Which is to say, perfect.

Makes 1 pie

1. Make the dough and refrigerate it for at least an hour, or overnight. Roll out the bottom crust and place it in a 9- to 10-inch pie plate. Tuck the crust into the plate and trim the edges. Refrigerate the crust while you prepare the next steps of the recipe.

2. In a small saucepan, combine the honey and ginger and warm it over low heat for 20 minutes. This will scent the honey and allow it to flow more freely. While the honey is warming, peel, pit, and slice the peaches so they're about ¼ inch thick. Put the slices in a large bowl and add the lemon juice, cayenne, nutmeg, and salt. Pour in the warmed honey and ginger. Mix gently until the honey and spices are evenly distributed, then taste and adjust the flavors as needed. Gently stir in the flour and set the filling aside.

3. Preheat the oven to 425 degrees F.

4. Roll out the top crust and retrieve the bottom crust from the refrigerator.

continued

1 recipe any double-crust pie dough

¾ cup clover honey

2 tablespoons peeled and finely chopped fresh ginger

5 large, ripe peaches or nectarines (about 2 pounds)

Juice of ½ medium lemon (about 1½ tablespoons)

Pinch of cayenne

Pinch of ground nutmeg

Pinch of salt

5 to 6 tablespoons flour (depending on how juicy the peaches are)

2 tablespoons chilled unsalted butter, cut into small pieces

Egg white wash (1 egg white beaten with 1 teaspoon water)

Demerara sugar, for sprinkling

5. Using a slotted spoon, put the peaches into the bottom crust. Pour in the juice, stopping about a ½ inch below the rim. Dot the filling with the butter, drape the top crust over it, trim the edges, and crimp or flute them. Cut generous steam vents, brush the crust with the egg white wash, and sprinkle it with the demerara sugar.

6. Bake the pie in the middle of the oven for 15 to 20 minutes, until the crust is blistered and blond. Reduce the heat to 375 degrees F and bake for 35 to 45 minutes more, rotating the pie front to back about halfway through to ensure even baking, until the crust is golden and the juices start to bubble slowly at the edges.

7. Cool on a wire rack for at least an hour before serving. Serve warm or at room temperature. Store leftovers on the kitchen counter loosely wrapped in a towel for up to 3 days.

❧ WHITE PEACH AND RASPBERRY GALETTE ❧

White peaches have a sweeter, higher, purer flavor than yellow peaches, though yellow peaches work equally well in this recipe. Raspberries tart things up a bit. Lillet, a French aperitif, and Portuguese vinho verde wine are summer drinks that add an optional floral note to the filling and also pair well with a thick slice of this juicy galette, best made in a cast-iron pan.

Makes 1 galette

1. Make the dough. Let it rest in the refrigerator for an hour while you prepare the next steps of the recipe.

2. If the peaches are very fuzzy, skin them before slicing. The easiest way is to dip them in boiling water for 10 seconds and then shock them in an ice bath. The peels will shred from the fruit with just a little rubbing. If the peaches have toothsome skins, leave them on. Slice them ¼ inch thick and put them in a medium bowl. Add half of the raspberries, the honey (½ cup if the peaches are quite sweet, ¾ cup if they aren't, or if you like a sweeter pie), lemon juice, salt, nutmeg, and Lillet. Taste and adjust the flavors as needed. Gently stir in the flour and butter, and set the filling aside.

3. Preheat the oven to 450 degrees F.

4. Retrieve the dough from the refrigerator. On a floured surface, roll it out into about an ⅛-inch-thick round. It will be large—14 inches, maybe bigger. (The dough doesn't need to be perfectly round, but it lays better in the pan if it is roundish.)

continued

1 recipe Galette Dough (page 70)

3 large, ripe white peaches (about 1½ pounds)

2 cups (1 pint) fresh rasp-berries, divided

½ to ¾ cup floral-tasting honey

Juice of ½ medium lemon (about 1½ tablespoons)

Pinch of salt

Big pinch of ground nutmeg

Splash of Lillet or vinho verde (optional)

5 to 6 tablespoons flour (depending on how juicy the peaches are)

2 tablespoons chilled unsalted butter, cut into small pieces

Egg white wash (1 egg white beaten with 1 teaspoon water)

Demerara sugar, for sprinkling

Trim the edges or patch the dough as needed to make it more round. Fold the dough into fourths, transfer it to the pan, and unfold it, tucking the dough gently into the edges of the pan. Let the excess drape over the edge of the pan.

5. Pour the filling into the dough and smooth it into a mound with your fingers. Sprinkle the rest of the raspberries over the top. Grab some of the excess dough and pull it toward the center of the galette. Grab another spot about three or four inches down and pull it toward the center, continuing until you have used all the dough to create a soft ruffle of crust surrounding the fruit in the center. Brush the dough with the egg white wash, and sprinkle it with the demerara sugar.

6. Bake the galette in the middle of the oven on a rimmed baking sheet for 10 to 15 minutes, until the crust is blistered and blond. Reduce the heat to 350 degrees F and bake for 40 to 50 minutes more, rotating the galette front to back about halfway through to ensure even baking, until the crust is deeply golden and the juices bubble slowly at the galette's edge.

7. Cool on a wire rack for at least an hour. Serve warm or at room temperature. Store leftovers on the kitchen counter loosely wrapped in a towel for up to 3 days.

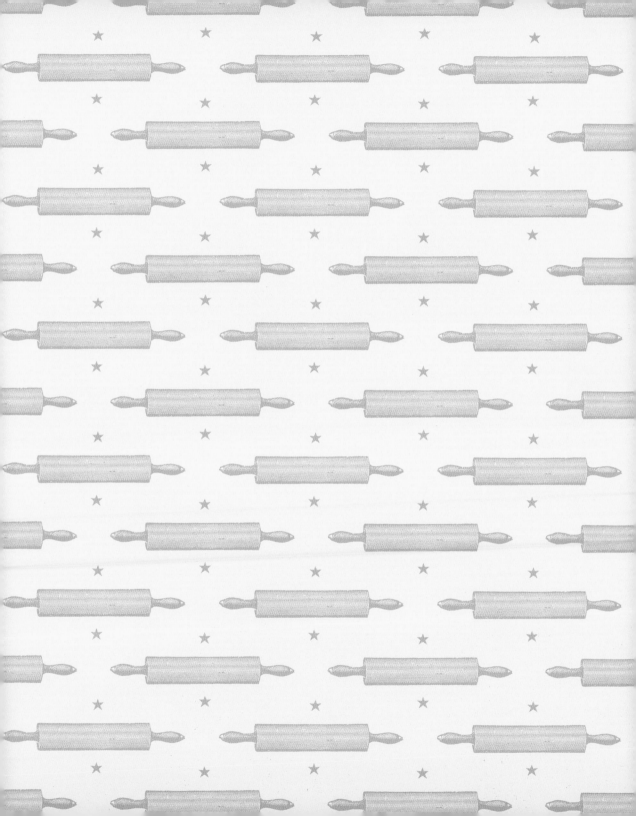

a tyranny of plums

Forgive me

they were delicious . . .

—WILLIAM CARLOS WILLIAMS

★　★　★　★　★

I'm in love with a plum. A different plum than you might find stacked in candescent magenta and yellow piles at the grocery store. My plum's skin is deep purple with a blue beard that rubs off beneath your thumb. It's yellow-fleshed and firm, too plump and cleft to be exactly almond-shaped, about the size of a skinny apricot. It pits easily. Each half is small enough that the side of a fork can cut it just once before it's bisected, bite-size.

Italian plum trees are as common to Seattle backyards as crazy uncles are to family reunions. Not everyone has one, but everyone knows someone who has one. If you have a plum tree (or as I once did, three), come August you experience what I call a "tyranny of plums." More than you can jam. More than you can freeze. More than will fit in twenty pies.

You call your friends. Out of guilt, kindness, or practicality (windfall plums make a terrible mess), whatever the reason, you call them. You visit for a while, then you send them home with heavy sacks of purple fruit. You pick sacks of your own to simmer into jam, to freeze, to make pie. After two weeks of this, you begin to curse the tree. You weren't always the sort of person who spends her days making jam. You remember your old life. You were free. Sometimes you threw out unfinished fruit and felt only a little ashamed. Sometimes you ate peaches. You can see that life waiting for you at the bottom of the last sack of plums.

If you're in a baking mood, choose Italian plums, also called Italian prune plums. Their firm texture and semitartness make them ideal for pie, better than their more bombastic supermarket cousins. If you can't find them, use the supermarket cousins. They'll bake up sweeter, with a softer texture, and they're just fine. If possible, I pick pluots over plums. Their apricot ancestors give them a little complexity that's welcome in a galette or pie. That's also true of apriums, which share pluot's parentage but in reverse ratio, more apricot than plum, which means they're firm, tart, and velvety when baked. Whatever you choose, make sure they're good and ripe by leaving them on the counter, not in the icebox, before you turn them into pie. Raw, some prefer them "so sweet and so cold," as William Carlos Williams wrote. Until time and repetition intervenes, I'll eat them at any temperature.

⁂ PLUM THYME PIE ⁂

This open-faced pie (it works wonderfully as a galette too) was inspired by a small batch of plum-thyme jam, the sleeper hit of a canning marathon that also included plum ginger, plum bourbon, and plum vanilla. Thyme pushes Italian plums toward their savory side. As a jam its sweet herbiness accompanies brie and crackers with polite confidence. As a pie, it is barely sweet, not so much an indulgence as a rightful part of the meal.

Makes 1 pie

1. Make the dough. Roll out the bottom crust and place it in a 9- to 9½-inch plate. Tuck the crust into the plate, trim the edges, and fold them into a ridge. Refrigerate the crust while you prepare the next steps of the recipe.

2. Preheat the oven to 425 degrees F.

3. In a large bowl combine the plums with the honey, lemon juice, thyme, butter, and salt. Taste and adjust the flavors as needed. Gently stir in the flour and set the filling aside.

4. Retrieve the bottom crust from the refrigerator. Arrange the plums inside the dough in snug concentric circles, starting at the edge and working your way in. Pour the remaining liquid, if there is any, over the top.

5. Bake the pie in the middle of the oven for 10 to 15 minutes, until the crust is blistered and blond. Reduce the heat to 350 degrees F and bake for 40 to 50 minutes more, until the crust is golden and the juices bubble slowly at the pie's edge.

6. Cool on a wire rack for at least an hour. Serve warm or at room temperature, cut into wedges and accompanied by slightly sweetened whipped crème fraîche. Store leftovers on the kitchen counter loosely wrapped in a towel for up to 3 days.

½ recipe any double-crust pie dough (for a single crust)

5 cups (about 25 to 30 small) Italian prune plums halved lengthwise and pitted

½ cup honey

Juice of ½ medium lemon (about 1½ tablespoons)

1 teaspoon finely chopped fresh thyme leaves

2 tablespoons unsalted butter, melted

Pinch of salt

2 tablespoons flour

This pie's success showed me that what works in jam will very likely work in pie. Which means your experiments in ginger, bourbon, or vanilla are likely to yield hits as well.

❧ PLUOT AND ELDERFLOWER GALETTE ❧

Sweet, juicy pluots are straightforwardly delicious when fresh and uncomplicatedly jammy when baked. Add a swig of elderflower liqueur to introduce an unexpected floral note—or don't, and keep things simple. Using plums instead of, or in combination with, pluots works wonderfully too.

Makes 1 galette

1 recipe Galette Dough (page 70)

5 pluots, sliced ½ inch thick and pitted (about 4 cups)

¾ cup granulated sugar

Juice of ½ medium lemon (about 1½ tablespoons)

2 tablespoons St. Germain

Pinch of salt

¼ cup flour

2 tablespoons butter

Egg white wash (1 egg white beaten with 1 teaspoon water)

Demerara sugar, for sprinkling

1. Make the dough. Let it rest in the refrigerator for an hour while you prepare the next steps of the recipe.

2. In a medium bowl, combine the pluots with the granulated sugar, lemon juice, St. Germain, and salt. Taste and adjust the flavors as needed. Gently stir in the flour and butter and set the filling aside.

3. Preheat the oven to 450 degrees F.

4. Retrieve the dough from the refrigerator. On a floured surface, roll it out into about an ⅛-inch-thick round. It will be large—14 inches, maybe bigger. Fold the dough into fourths, transfer it to a medium cast-iron pan or 9-inch pie dish (or, alternately, unfold it onto a parchment paper–lined baking sheet to bake free-form), and unfold it, tucking the dough gently into the edges of the pan. Let the excess drape over the edge of the pan.

5. Mound the filling in the center of the dough, leaving 2 or 3 inches of dough bare around the edges. Grab some of the excess dough and pull it toward the center of the galette. Grab another spot about three or four inches down and pull it toward the center, continuing until you have used all the dough to create a soft ruffle of pleats surrounding the fruit in the center. Brush the dough with the egg white wash, and sprinkle it with the demerara sugar.

6. Bake the galette in the middle of the oven for 10 to 15 minutes, until the crust is blistered and blond. Reduce the heat to 350 degrees F. Bake for 40 to 50 minutes more, until the crust is deeply golden and the juices bubble slowly at the galette's edge.

7. Cool on a wire rack for at least an hour. Serve warm or at room temperature. Store leftovers on the kitchen counter loosely wrapped in a towel for up to 3 days.

⚜ LAVENDER APRIUM PIE ⚜

Something about this combination seems gratuitously soft, like Laura Ashley drapery.

Culinary lavender is light and creamy, as if it's anticipating being turned into lavender ice cream. Garden-variety lavender tastes like soap (so does culinary lavender if you use too much of it). Grow culinary lavender in your garden or buy it at fine cooking stores. (I found a tin of it at the Pelindaba Lavender Farm Store on San Juan Island, Washington.) Try it in anything you might use rosemary with; the two herbs are related.

Makes 1 pie

1 recipe any double-crust pie dough

5 cups (about 9) ripe apriums sliced ½ inch thick and pitted

1 teaspoon finely chopped culinary lavender

½ cup floral-tasting honey

½ cup granulated sugar

Juice of ½ medium lemon (about 1½ tablespoons)

Pinch of salt

5 tablespoons flour

2 tablespoons chilled unsalted butter, cut into small pieces

Egg white wash (1 egg beaten with 1 teaspoon water)

Demerara sugar, for sprinkling

1. Make the dough and refrigerate it for at least an hour, or overnight. Roll out the bottom crust and place it in a 9- or 10-inch pie plate. Tuck the crust into the plate and trim the edges. Refrigerate the crust while you prepare the next steps of the recipe.

2. Preheat the oven to 425 degrees F.

3. In a large bowl, gently combine the apriums with the lavender, honey, granulated sugar, lemon juice, and salt. Taste and adjust the flavors as needed. Gently stir in the flour and butter, and set the filling aside.

4. Roll out the top crust and retrieve the bottom crust from the refrigerator.

5. Mound the filling into the bottom crust, and drape the top crust over it. Trim, fold, and flute the edges if you like. Cut generous steam vents, brush the crust with the egg white wash, and sprinkle it with the demerara sugar.

6. Bake the pie in the middle of the oven for 15 to 20 minutes, until the crust is blistered and blond. Reduce the heat to 375 degrees F and bake for 35 to 45 minutes more, until the crust is deeply golden and the juices bubble slowly at the pie's edge.

7. Cool on a wire rack for at least an hour. Serve warm or at room temperature. Store leftovers on the kitchen counter loosely wrapped in a towel for up to 3 days.

❧ APRICOT, PLUM, AND RASPBERRY GALETTE *with* CHAMBORD GLAZE ❧

Adapt this recipe to any combination of stone fruit and berries that sounds delicious to you; you should have about 5 cups of sliced stone fruit in all. This recipe is written for a cast-iron pan or pie plate, but baking a free-form galette would be just as lovely. If you do that, reduce the amount of fruit—4 cups of stone fruit instead of 5—it will set up more cleanly. You can use Grand Marnier or St. Germain if you can't find Chambord.

Makes 1 galette

1 recipe Galette Dough (page 70)

8 ripe plums or pluots, sliced in thick wedges and pitted

4 ripe apricots or apriums, quartered (cut them so they are about the same size as the sliced plums) and pitted

½ cup fresh of frozen raspberries, plus a handful for the filling

½ cup granulated sugar

Juice of ½ medium lemon (about 1½ tablespoons)

Big pinch of salt

5 tablespoons flour

2 tablespoons chilled unsalted butter, cut into small pieces

5 tablespoons raspberry jam

1 tablespoon Chambord

Egg white wash (1 egg white beaten with 1 teaspoon water)

Demerara sugar, for sprinkling

1. Make the dough. Let it rest in the refrigerator for an hour while you prepare the next steps of the recipe.

2. In a medium bowl, combine the plums, apricots, a handful of raspberries, granulated sugar, lemon juice, and salt. Taste and adjust the flavors as needed. Gently mix in the flour and butter chunks and set the filling aside.

3. Preheat the oven to 450 degrees F.

4. To prepare the glaze, in a small saucepan over medium heat, mix the raspberry jam and Chambord. Bring them to a gentle boil, then remove the pan from the heat and set the glaze aside to cool.

5. Retrieve the dough from the refrigerator. On a floured surface, roll it out into about an ⅛-inch-thick round. It will be large—14 inches, maybe bigger. (The dough doesn't need to be perfectly round, but it lays better in the pan if it is roundish.) Trim the edges or patch the dough as needed to make it more round. Fold the dough into fourths, transfer it to the pan, and unfold it, tucking the dough gently into the edges of the pan. Let the excess drape over the edge of the pan.

6. Mound the filling into the dough, leaving at least 3 inches of dough bare around the edges. Arrange the remaining ½ cup of the raspberries in the center. Brush the glaze over everything. Grab some of the excess dough and pull it toward the center of the galette. Grab another spot about three or four inches down and pull it toward the center, continuing until you have used all the dough to create a soft ruffle of crust surrounding the fruit in the center. Brush the dough with the egg white wash, and sprinkle it with the demerara sugar.

7. Bake the galette in the middle of the oven for 10 to 15 minutes, until the crust is blistered and blond. Reduce the heat to 350 degrees F. Remove the galette from the oven and brush the glaze over the fruit. Bake for 40 to 50 minutes more, until the crust is deeply golden and the juices bubble slowly at the galette's edge.

8. Cool on a wire rack for at least an hour. Serve warm or at room temperature. Store leftovers on the kitchen counter loosely wrapped in a towel for up to 3 days.

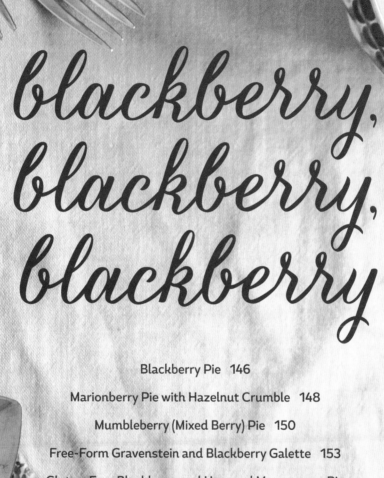

blackberry, blackberry, blackberry

There are moments when the body is as numinous

as words, days that are the good flesh continuing.

Such tenderness, those afternoons and evenings,

saying blackberry, blackberry, blackberry.

—"MEDITATION AT LAGUNITAS," ROBERT HASS

★ ★ ★ ★ ★

Find them in clear-cuts. By riversides and roadsides. In interstitial pieces of private or municipal land that, regardless of what the county might say, have no clear owner. Wild blackberry brambles are at home on land that's been disturbed from its natural condition but hasn't yet been tapped for human use. They're considered a noxious weed in my home state; anyone who says they're going to plant blackberries in their garden gets the raised eyebrow usually reserved for those intent on planting bamboo.

Invasive Himalayan blackberries are seedy and hairy, not ideal for eating fresh, though to many blackberry foragers, that hardly matters. When they ripen from bright magenta to dark purple-black, they call attention to the overlooked spaces they've settled, turning no-man's-lands into fresh fruit buffets. Even on some of Seattle's main roads it isn't out of the ordinary to see someone reach into a briar and pick a few berries while they wait for the bus. My own blackberry ritual involved driving to North Seattle with friends, out where the sidewalk ends, to find good picking. We looked for berries that fell easily into our hands—a sure sign of ripeness. Blackberries don't ripen off the cane, so picking the stubborn ones is sour exercise. We'd come home dirty and scratched, happy as snails in a lettuce bed.

★ ★ ★ ★ ★

Cultivated blackberries have finer flavors and textures, gentler seeds and balder sides. Marionberries are sweeter, juicier, with a trace of vanilla. They're champions of the freezer, losing no quality when packed well, making marionberry pie as welcome a treat in February as it is in August. Boysenberries and olallieberries are plump, quite large blackberry varieties. Loganberries and tayberries are the offspring of raspberries and blackberries. All make excellent pie and behave similarly when cooked—collapsing into pulp and juice, speckled with seeds, requiring a stiff dose of thickener. Their sweetness is best framed by lemon, while their underlying tartness often requires a full cup of sugar to be tamed. Like apples, blackberry varieties gain much when a sweet variety is baked with a tart variety. When choosing a carton, find one that isn't leaking juice (which is a possible sign of overripeness) or furred with mold, which can set in if the berries have been kept in less than ideal conditions, and taste a berry to judge their sweetness or tartness. Use your berries quickly, even if you've refrigerated them. About the end of blackberries, the late Seamus Heaney said it best: "Each year I hoped they'd keep, knew they would not."

⚜ BLACKBERRY PIE ⚜

This is one of the most easily made and simply satisfying pies out there. To enhance the texture of frozen berries, smash some of them up a bit with the edge of a wooden spoon, just enough so broken drupelets will cushion the whole berries, creating a filling that's neither all jam nor individual berries, but somewhere in the middle and just right.

Makes 1 pie

1 recipe any double-crust pie dough

5 cups (about 2 pounds) any variety fresh or frozen blackberries

1 cup granulated sugar

Juice of ½ medium lemon (about 1½ tablespoons)

Big pinch of ground nutmeg

Pinch of salt

5 to 6 tablespoons flour (depending on how juicy the berries are)

2 tablespoons well-chilled unsalted butter, cut into small pieces

Egg white wash (1 egg white beaten with 1 teaspoon water)

Demerara sugar, for sprinkling

1. Make the dough and refrigerate it for at least an hour, or overnight. Roll out the bottom crust and place it in a 9- to 10-inch pie plate. Tuck the crust into the plate and trim the edges. Refrigerate the crust while you prepare the next steps of the recipe.

2. Preheat the oven to 425 degrees F.

3. In a large bowl, mix the blackberries with the granulated sugar, lemon juice, nutmeg, and salt. Taste and adjust the flavors as needed. Stir in the flour, smashing some of the berries as you do so if you're using frozen ones. Set the filling aside.

4. Roll out the top crust and retrieve the bottom crust from the refrigerator.

5. Pour the filling into the bottom crust and smooth it into a mound with your hand. Dot the filling with the butter. Drape the top crust over it, trim the edges, and crimp or flute them. Cut generous steam vents, brush the crust with the egg white wash, and sprinkle it with the demerara sugar.

6. Bake the pie in the middle of the oven for 15 to 20 minutes, until the crust is blond and blistered. Rotate the pie front to back and reduce the heat to 375 degrees F. Bake about 35 to 45 minutes more, until the crust is deeply golden and the juices bubble slowly at the pie's edge.

7. Cool on a wire rack for at least an hour. Serve warm or at room temperature. Store leftovers on the kitchen counter loosely wrapped in a towel for up to 3 days.

❧ MARIONBERRY PIE
with HAZELNUT CRUMBLE ❧

Oregon produces 99 percent of the US hazelnut crop and is the home state of the marion-berry. This pie pairs two crown jewels of the Pacific Northwest harvest.

Makes 1 pie

½ recipe any double-crust pie dough (for a single crust)

For the filling:

5 cups (about 2 pounds) fresh or frozen marionberries

½ cup sugar

Juice of ½ medium lemon (about 1½ tablespoons)

Big pinch of ground nutmeg

Pinch of salt

4 to 5 tablespoons tapioca flour (depending on how juicy the berries are)

For the crumble topping:

¾ cup hazelnuts

½ cup flour

½ cup sugar

½ teaspoon salt

6 tablespoons chilled unsalted butter, cut into ½-tablespoon-size pieces

1. Make the dough and refrigerate it for at least an hour, or overnight. Roll out the bottom crust and place it in a 9- to 10-inch pie plate. Tuck the crust into the plate, trim the edges, and fold them into a ridge. Freeze the crust while you prepare the next steps of the recipe.

2. Preheat the oven to 425 degrees F.

3. To make the filling, in a large bowl, gently combine the marionberries, sugar, lemon juice, nutmeg, and salt. Taste and adjust the flavors as needed. Gently stir in the tapioca flour and set the filling aside.

4. To make the topping, put the hazelnuts, flour, sugar, and salt in the bowl of a food processor and pulse until the nuts are well chopped. Add the butter and process again in 1-second pulses until the mixture resembles fine crumbs.

5. Retrieve the bottom crust from the freezer. Pour the filling into the bottom crust and smooth it into a mound with your hand. With your hands, crumble some of the topping into small globes (for aesthetic effect). Spread the topping over the fruit in a thick, even layer.

6. Bake the pie in the middle of the oven for 10 to 15 minutes until the crust is blistered and blond. Reduce the heat to 375 degrees F and bake for about 50 minutes more, until the topping has browned and the juices bubble slowly at the pie's edge. If the topping is browning too quickly, tent it with aluminum foil.

7. Cool on a wire rack for at least an hour. Serve warm or at room temperature. Store leftovers on the kitchen counter loosely wrapped in a towel for up to 3 days.

❧ MUMBLEBERRY (MIXED BERRY) PIE ❧

A mumbleberry pie is a berry mixed with any other berry that creates a combination so delicious it stops all conversation. Choose as many different kinds of berries as you like—even non-berries like peaches, apples, and rhubarb can be sneaked in—as long as the overall quantity of fruit is 5 to 6 cups. See "How to Be Fruitful" (page 44) to get the perfect amount for your pie plate and "How to Keep Your Cool" (page 45) for tips on baking with frozen fruit.

Makes 1 pie

1 recipe any double-crust pie dough

1 cup each of 5 different fresh or frozen berries (blueberry, blackberry, marionberry, boysenberry, raspberry, strawberry, etc.)

1 cup granulated sugar

Juice of 1 medium lemon (2 to 3 tablespoons)

Pinch of salt

¼ cup to ⅓ cup flour, depending on how juicy the berries are

2 tablespoons chilled unsalted butter, cut into small pieces

Egg white wash (1 egg white beaten with 1 teaspoon water)

Demerara sugar, for sprinkling

1. Make the dough and refrigerate it for at least an hour, or overnight. Roll out the bottom crust and place it in a 9- to 10-inch pie plate. Tuck the crust into the plate and trim the edges. Refrigerate the crust while you prepare the next steps of the recipe.

2. Preheat the oven to 425 degrees F.

3. In a large bowl, gently mix the berries with the granulated sugar, lemon juice, and salt. Taste and adjust the flavors as needed. Gently stir in the flour and set the filling aside.

4. Roll out the top crust and retrieve the bottom crust from the refrigerator.

5. Pour the filling into the bottom crust, mound it with your hands, and dot it with the butter. Drape the top crust over it. Trim, fold, and flute the edges if you like. Cut generous steam vents, brush the crust with the egg white wash, and sprinkle it with the demerara sugar.

6. Bake the pie in the middle of the oven for 15 to 20 minutes, until the crust is blond and blistered. Rotate the pie front to back and reduce the heat to 375 degrees F. Bake for 35 to 45 minutes more, until the crust is deeply golden and the juices bubble slowly at the pie's edge.

7. Cool the pie on a wire rack for at least an hour before serving. Store leftovers on the kitchen counter loosely wrapped in a towel for up to 3 days.

Try replacing half of the thickener and 1 cup of the fruit with a grated apple.

❖ FREE-FORM GRAVENSTEIN AND
BLACKBERRY GALETTE ❖

Blackberries cushion their firm core and stubborn seeds in fat, juicy, purple-black drupelets that burst delicate and sweet if they're perfectly ripe or tough and sour if they aren't. Gravensteins are a late summer apple with a soft tartness I crave all year. Sliced, baked, and stacked in a pie, they soften until they're barely held together at the peel, yet somehow keep their shape and texture—never mushy, never bland. They're my favorite pie apple. In the Pacific Northwest, they make an appearance at farmers' markets around the same time as we start picking blackberries from their roadside canes. If you can't find Gravensteins, substitute a tart baking apple like Cortland, Macoun, Akane, or (as a last resort) Granny Smith.

Makes 1 galette

1. Make the dough. Let it rest in the refrigerator for an hour while you prepare the next steps of the recipe.

2. Core the apples and slice them thinly, about ⅛ of an inch. A note on peeling: unless the apple skin is unusually thick or blighted in some way, I never peel. If you prefer to peel, don't let me stop you. Peel away. The recipe won't change a bit.

3. Put the apple slices in a medium bowl and squeeze the lemon juice over them to prevent browning. Add the blackberries, granulated sugar, salt, and nutmeg. Stir to combine. Taste and adjust the flavors as needed. Stir in the flour and butter, and set the filling aside.

4. Preheat the oven to 450 degrees F.

continued

1 recipe Galette Dough (page 70)

1 large or 2 medium Gravenstein apples

Juice of ½ medium lemon plus one more squeeze from the other half (about 2 tablespoons)

1 to 2 cups (½ pint to 1 pint) blackberries

¾ cup granulated sugar

Pinch of salt

Pinch of ground nutmeg

3 tablespoons flour

2 tablespoons chilled unsalted butter, cut into small pieces

Egg white wash (1 egg white beaten with 1 teaspoon water)

Demerara sugar, for sprinkling

I've had the best luck with this galette when I don't pack it too full of fruit. Just over half a pint of blackberries is perfect, and you should have about 2 to 3 cups sliced apples. Four to five cups of fruit (depending on how large your Gravensteins are, or how many pints blackberries you'd like to add) is just right. Err closer to 4.

5. Retrieve the dough from the refrigerator. On a floured surface, roll it out into about an ⅛-inch-thick round. It will be large, 14 to 16 inches. Fold the dough into fourths and lay it in the center of a rimmed baking sheet that has been lined with parchment paper (not waxed paper, which will smoke).

6. Mound the filling in the middle of the dough, leaving 2 to 3 inches of dough bare around the edges, and dot the filling with the butter. (Mound the fruit high if you have to; it will bake down.) Grab some of the excess dough and pull it toward the center of the galette. Grab another spot about 3 or 4 inches down and pull it toward the center, continuing until you have used all the dough to create a soft ruffle of crust surrounding the fruit in the center. Brush the dough with the egg white wash, and sprinkle it with the demerara sugar.

7. Bake the galette in the middle of the oven for 10 to 15 minutes, until the crust is blistered and blond. Reduce the heat to 350 degrees F and bake for another 40 to 50 minutes more, until the crust is golden and the juices bubble slowly at the galette's edge.

8. Let the galette cool for 20 minutes, then transfer it to a serving platter or cutting board by picking up the galette, including the parchment paper, placing it on the platter, and pulling the parchment from beneath the galette. If juices have leaked out, they may adhere to the paper. Gently peel it away to prevent tearing.

9. Cool the galette for another 20 to 30 minutes or so, until it's barely warm. Store leftovers on the kitchen counter loosely covered in a towel for up to 3 days.

✣ GLUTEN-FREE BLACKBERRY AND HONEYED MASCARPONE PIE
with ALMOND FLOUR CRUST ✣

A rich yet simple frame for fresh blackberries, or any other high-quality fresh berry. Use the very best you can find. Layered atop honeyed cream, there's nowhere for bad fruit to hide.

Makes 1 pie

1. Prepare the crust and set it aside on a wire rack to cool completely while you make the filling.

2. In a medium bowl, combine the mascarpone and sour cream with an electric hand mixer. Add the honey, vanilla, and salt. Spoon the filling into the cooled piecrust, smooth the top with a spatula, and sprinkle the nutmeg over the top. Arrange the blackberries in concentric rings atop the filling, covering it completely. Serve chilled. Cover and refrigerate any leftovers.

1 recipe Gluten-Free Almond Flour Piecrust (page 75)

⅔ cup mascarpone cheese

½ cup sour cream

⅓ cup clover honey

½ teaspoon vanilla extract

Pinch of salt

Large pinch of ground nutmeg

1 to 2 cups fresh blackberries

> To get really DIY, strain a pint of plain, full-fat Greek yogurt through cheesecloth or a fine sieve for 24 hours. The whey will drip out, leaving a rich, thick cream much like mascarpone, but tangier. A pint yields about 1⅓ cups of yogurt-cheese and ⅔ cup of whey. Substitute the yogurt-cheese for all the mascarpone and sour cream in this recipe. Discard the whey.

❖ HUCKLEBERRY PIE ❖

Huckleberry pie is as precious a treat as the chance to go foraging with a friend on a hot August day. This version uses vanilla extract and a slug of bourbon to enhance the richness of the berries, but you could easily do without them, using only lemon, sugar, and a little nutmeg to flavor the filling. The juice cooks down into a syrupy sauce you'll lick from the plate, not wanting to waste a drop.

Makes 1 pie

1 recipe any double-crust pie dough

4 cups (2 pints) fresh or frozen huckleberries

1 cup granulated sugar

Juice of ½ medium lemon (about 1½ tablespoons)

½ teaspoon vanilla extract

2 tablespoons bourbon

Big pinch of salt

¼ cup flour

2 tablespoons chilled unsalted butter, cut into small pieces

Egg white wash (1 egg white beaten with 1 teaspoon water)

Demerara sugar, for sprinkling

1. Make the dough and refrigerate it for at least an hour, or overnight. Roll out the bottom crust and place it in a 9- to 9½-inch pie plate. Tuck the crust into the plate and trim the edges. Refrigerate the crust while you prepare the next steps of the recipe.

2. Preheat the oven to 425 degrees F.

3. In a medium bowl, combine the huckleberries with the granulated sugar, lemon juice, vanilla, bourbon, and salt. Taste and adjust the flavors as needed. Stir in the flour and set the filling aside.

4. Roll out the top crust and retrieve the bottom crust from the refrigerator.

5. Pour the filling into the bottom crust and smooth it into a mound with your hands. Dot the filling with the butter. Drape the top crust over it, trim the edges, and crimp or flute them. Cut generous steam vents, brush the crust with the egg white wash, and sprinkle it with the demerara sugar.

6. Bake the pie in the middle of the oven for 15 to 20 minutes, until the crust is blond and blistered. Rotate the pie front to back and reduce the heat to 375 degrees F. Bake for 35 to 45 minutes more, until the crust is deeply golden and the juices bubble slowly at the pie's edge.

7. Cool on a wire rack for at least an hour. Serve warm or at room temperature. Store leftovers on the kitchen counter loosely wrapped in a towel for up to 3 days.

foraging for huckleberries

Not a blackberry at all, nor related to them, huckleberries ripen in the wild around the same time as blackberries and exude a dark-purple juice that stubbornly stains fingers and tongues. They've been impossible to domesticate, so they remain a treat for birds, bears, and human foragers on the mountainsides of the Pacific Northwest and Montana.

To find enough to make a pie, I hiked with a friend into the forest around Mount St. Helens, where a 1932 handshake between Chief Yallup and the Gifford Pinchot National Forest supervisor reserved part of the Sawtooth Berry Fields for the Yakama Nation. A park ranger was careful to point us toward the public's berry fields, and told us to drive down unmarked forest service roads for the best picking.

Spindly and knee-high, huckleberry bushes grow in patches of sunlight created by downed logs and at road edges, where sun can break through the thick forest canopy. We followed a trail of bushes, bending down every now and then as if to talk to a small child—at that lower angle, berries hidden under fans of flat leaves suddenly revealed themselves. Each berry was small but fat, about half the size of a cultivated blueberry, and so sour. An afternoon of picking yielded six cups. Extra berries froze perfectly for later pies.

an everlasting apple pie

Good apple pies are a considerable part
of our domestic happiness.

—JANE AUSTEN

★ ★ ★ ★ ★

Apple season spans the heat of late summer and the shelter-taking of fall, so apple pie contains the warmth of an autumn kitchen and the memory of summer's last blaze, a reminder that shelter's comfort is defined by our need for it. Without rain and sleet and snow, we'd never share the joy of huddling around a fire. We'd never know what it means to truly "come in from the cold."

Apple's natural pectin and sturdy, sliceable structure make apple pie one of the easiest double-crust creations to get right on the first try.

The first task is to choose apples—pie apples, preferably, which are tart and firm, often heirloom, and best found at farms, farmers' markets, and well-stocked produce aisles. The best of them all is the green-skinned Gravenstein, a late-summer variety with a short season. Its tart taste is more complex and better framed by sugar and spice than, say, a sweet Gala; its cells are smaller, with stronger cell walls, unlike the delicate water-ballooney cells of apples bred to crunch and juice and please with sweetness. Gravenstein cells soften with baking yet keep their shape. An eating apple, on the other hand, will become unexciting mush or the opposite, as with Pink Ladies, and never quite bake all the way through, though the pie is clearly done. Other pie apples are Akane, Cortland, Northern Spy, Ginger Gold, Macoun, and Winesap, to name just a handful. If all you can find is McIntosh and Granny Smith, those will work perfectly fine.

Apples keep amazingly well; I'll buy two boxes in late summer/early fall and work through them all fall. That said, apples' sturdiness can create an illusion of constant seasonality—don't believe it. July apples are old apples, and they won't bake or taste nearly as good. In fact, from April until the first apple crops, I quit apple pie altogether. Which has the added bonus of making that first apple pie of the season a ritual worth gathering family for.

Choose two varieties of apples for your pies—my favorites are Akane and Gravenstein on the West Coast, and Cortland and Ginger Gold on the East. Their strengths will complement each other. One last secret: slip one or two ripe pears into the mix, and don't tell. They'll create a range of flavor that's hard to describe, a cognitive dissonance that takes like magic.

It depends on how big the apples are, but I find that usually three of one type, two of another, plus one pear is plenty enough to fill a pie plate. You can get away with piling apples mile-high—eight cups, even nine are possible. The trick is to thinly slice the apples, press them gently down on the filling once it's piled in the bottom crust to reduce air holes, and pour the liquid part of the filling (juices and honey, usually) only after the apples are in the pie plate, and only so the liquid reaches ½ inch below the rim of the pie, no more.

Its high pectin means apple pie needs only two or three tablespoons of flour and butter each to thicken. The juice will behave a little differently than that of a berry or stone-fruit pie. It may appear a little watery at the edges, rather than viscous. That's okay. You'll know the pie is done when a knife inserted into the filling through a vent easily pierces them. As the pie cools, the thin juices will firm up beautifully.

❖ APPLE PIE ❖

Apple pies are easy to invent. Start with this basic recipe and fiddle at will, adding other fruit, spices, and sweeteners. In fact, most of the recipes in this section began with this simple template. I use a food processor fitted with the slicing disc to cut my apples as thinly as possible (⅛ inch). Core them, but don't peel them (unless you want to).

Makes 1 pie

1. Make the dough and refrigerate it for at least an hour, or overnight. Roll out the bottom crust and place it in a 9- to 10-inch pie plate. Tuck the crust into the plate and trim the edges. Refrigerate the crust while you prepare the next steps of the recipe.

2. Preheat the oven to 425 degrees F.

3. Put the apple and pear slices in a large bowl and squeeze the lemon juice over them to prevent browning. Stir in the granulated sugar, cinnamon, nutmeg, and salt. Taste and adjust the flavors as needed. Stir in the flour and set the filling aside.

4. Roll out the top crust and retrieve the bottom crust from the refrigerator.

5. Using a slotted spoon, put the apples in the bottom crust, pressing them down gently to pack them into the pie. Pour the liquid from the filling over the apples and dot the filling with the butter. Drape the top crust over it, trim the edges, and crimp or flute them. Cut generous steam vents, brush the crust with the egg white wash, and sprinkle it with the demerara sugar.

continued

1 recipe any double-crust pie dough

3 Gravenstein or Granny Smith apples, peeled if desired, cored, and thinly sliced

2 Akane, Ginger Gold, or McIntosh apples, peeled if desired, cored, and thinly sliced

1 any variety ripe pear, cored, and thinly sliced

Juice of ½ medium lemon, or more (1 to 2 tablespoons)

¾ cup granulated sugar

½ teaspoon ground cinnamon

¼ teaspoon ground nutmeg

Big pinch of salt

3 tablespoons flour

2 tablespoons chilled unsalted butter, cut into small pieces

Egg white wash (1 egg white beaten with 1 teaspoon water)

Demerara sugar, for sprinkling

6. Bake the pie in the middle of the oven for 15 to 20 minutes, until the crust is blond and blistered. Rotate the pie front to back and reduce the heat to 375 degrees F. Bake for 35 to 45 minutes more, until the crust is deeply golden and the juices bubble slowly at the pie's edge.

7. Cool on a wire rack for at least an hour. Serve warm or at room temperature. Store leftovers on the kitchen counter loosely wrapped in a towel for up to 3 days.

what does it mean to be american as apple pie?

*Pie is the American synonym of prosperity and
its varying contents the calendar of the changing
seasons. Pie is the food of the heroic. No pie-eating
people can ever be permanently vanquished.*

—NEW YORK TIMES, MAY 3, 1902

What does it mean to be American as apple pie? Some trace the connection to the legend of Johnny Appleseed, who prepared the West for settlement by planting apple trees wherever he wandered. Some trace it to the apple orchards of colonial America, how apple cider was at one time safer to drink than water, how its edible container of pastry made apple pie a practical choice for schoolchildren and field-workers. Pie is a treat of European origin, brought over by colonialists and adapted to suit the so-called New World. We didn't invent pie; we invented *American* pie.

"Mom and apple pie" is slang for "something good and right we can all agree on," gifted to American English by soldiers during World War II, who supposedly used this as a stock answer for why they went to war. "American as motherhood and apple pie" was the next—and most audacious—version of the phrase. Staking national claim to motherhood suggests we can make something American simply by saying that it is.

My impulse is to complicate the phrase, apply it to things that are less stereo-typical, less nationalistic. To make the cliché interesting again is to play with what American and apple pie can be. John Lehndorff, former executive director of the American Pie Council, puts it well: "When you say that something is 'as American as apple pie,' what you're really saying is that the item came to this country from

continued

elsewhere and was transformed into a distinctly American experience." The cliché can signal what it attempts to conceal: there is nothing easy about presuming what American means, then or now.

We expect apple pie to be a comfort, not a challenge. It reminds us of a time when all food was homemade, when "just like Grandma used to make" wasn't a useful advertising slogan because Grandma actually used to make . . . whatever it was. But the slogan has been used to sell food since the late 1800s—far before our grandmothers' time—which means the only thing true about that truism is how much we want to eat food made with love. That's nostalgia at work, whitewashing the past.

Nostalgia's etymology is *homecoming* layered with *ache*. It's the thing that defines Americana—an attraction to things past, a longing for simpler, better times that may not have ever existed. Apple pie makes nostalgia edible.

Therein lies its genius. As a crown relic of Americana, apple pie doesn't have to be novel to be interesting, which is saying something for a culture obsessed with all things new. While its cultural importance can be generalized by cliché, its culinary importance is sincere: apple pie reminds us that homemade food sustains us in deep, hard-to-describe ways. The time and skill it takes to make a pie shows us that we are cared for. That it's not about having time, but about making it. Through the rituals of language and dessert, what apple pie *was* is also what it *is*: homespun, authentic, and humble, a food that uses the fruits of harvest while symbolizing the agricultural roots of our nation, a sweet that satisfies like a meal, nurturing while it treats.

❖ BRANDIED APPLE
AND CRACKED CARDAMOM PIE ❖

This pie was created in collaboration with Sara Fisher, who mixes the best drinks in town at two fantastic Seattle bars. The cocktail is made with Applejack, rye whiskey, maraschino liqueur, and cardamom bitters, and called "Falling Fruit" for the curls of lemon and orange zest that float just beneath the surface of the liquor. If you visit her at Hazlewood or The Hideout and order our cocktail, remember to say hi for me.

Makes 1 pie

1. Make the dough and refrigerate it for at least an hour, or overnight. Roll out the bottom crust and place it in a 9- to 10-inch pie plate. Tuck the crust into the plate and trim the edges. Refrigerate the crust while you prepare the next steps of the recipe.

2. Preheat the oven to 425 degrees F.

3. In a small saucepan over medium-low heat, warm the honey, granulated sugar, and cardamom until the sugar has dissolved and the honey is liquid. Put the apples in a large bowl and add the brandy, salt, and nutmeg. Pour the honey mixture in and stir gently to combine. Taste and adjust the flavors as needed. Add another glug of brandy if you like. Stir in the flour and set the filling aside.

4. Roll out the top crust and retrieve the bottom crust from the refrigerator.

continued

1 recipe any double-crust pie dough

½ cup honey

¼ cup granulated sugar

½ teaspoon freshly cracked cardamom seeds

5 or 6 (about 2 pounds) tart pie apples, peeled if desired, cored, and thinly sliced

2 to 3 tablespoons Applejack brandy

Pinch of salt

Pinch of ground nutmeg

3 tablespoons flour

2 tablespoons chilled unsalted butter, cut into small pieces

Egg white wash (1 egg white beaten with 1 teaspoon water)

Demerara sugar, for sprinkling

To re-create the kick of cardamom bitters, use a spice grinder to make jagged chunks of cardamom seed. If you can't find cardamom seeds, you may need to buy the pods and pop the seeds out yourself. The idea is to have brief, almost bitter tastes of cardamom punctuate the soothing sweetness of honey. If you can't find cardamom seeds, or if momentary bitterness isn't your idea of dessert, substitute ¼ teaspoon finely ground cardamom for the chunkier seeds. I like to use two kinds of apples in this recipe, such as Gravenstein, Akane, Macoun, Cortland, Jonathan, or McIntosh.

5. Using a slotted spoon, put the apples in the bottom crust, pressing them down gently to pack them into the pie. Pour in the liquid from the filling, stopping about a ½ inch below the rim. Smooth the filling into a mound with your hands and dot it with the butter. Drape the top crust over it, trim the edges, and crimp or flute them. Cut generous steam vents, brush the crust with the egg white wash, and sprinkle it with the demerara sugar.

6. Bake the pie in the middle of the oven for 15 to 20 minutes, until the crust is blond and blistered. Rotate the pie front to back and reduce the heat to 375 degrees F. Bake for 35 to 45 minutes more, until the crust is deeply golden and the juices bubble slowly at the pie's edge.

7. Cool on a wire rack for at least an hour. Serve warm or at room temperature. Store leftovers on the kitchen counter loosely wrapped in a towel for up to 3 days.

⚜ CHEDDAR-CRUSTED APPLE PIE ⚜

The old bromide goes "An apple pie without the cheese is like a kiss without the squeeze." This pie was inspired by a recipe from Ken Haedrich's incomparable *Pie*.

=== *Makes 1 pie* ===

1. Make the dough and refrigerate it for at least an hour, or overnight. Roll out the bottom crust and place it in a 9- to 10-inch pie plate. Tuck the crust into the plate and trim the edges. Refrigerate the crust while you prepare the next steps of the recipe.

2. Preheat the oven to 425 degrees F.

3. In a large bowl, mix the apples with the sugar, lemon juice, and salt. Taste and adjust flavors as necessary. Mix in flour. Set the filling aside.

4. Roll out the top crust and retrieve the bottom crust from the refrigerator.

5. Pour the filling into the bottom crust and smooth it into a mound with your hands. Dot the top of the filling with butter. Drape the top crust over the filling, trim the edges, and crimp or flute them. Cut generous steam vents, brush the crust with the egg white wash, and sprinkle it with a little salt.

continued

1 recipe Cheese Crust (page 68), made with cheddar

5 or 6 (about 2 pounds) tart pie apples, peeled if desired, cored, and thinly sliced

⅓ cup sugar

2 teaspoons freshly squeezed lemon juice

Pinch of salt

3 tablespoons flour

2 tablespoons chilled unsalted butter, cut into small pieces

Egg white wash (1 egg white beaten with 1 teaspoon water)

Coarse salt

6. Bake the pie in the middle of the oven for 15 to 20 minutes, until the crust is blond and blistered. Rotate the pie front to back and reduce the heat to 375 degrees F. Bake for 35 to 45 minutes more, until the crust is deeply golden and the juices bubble slowly at the pie's edge.

7. Cool on a wire rack for at least an hour. Serve warm or at room temperature. Store leftovers on the kitchen counter loosely wrapped in a towel for up to 3 days.

❖ WHISKEY CRUMBLE APPLE PIE ❖

I'm not usually a fan of crumble-top pies, but Jen Bervin and Ron Silver's whiskey crumble apple pie slayed me, then revived me, then made me a crumble believer. Their book *Bubby's Homemade Pies* is full of fantastic recipes, but this one's based on my hands-down (and hands-on) favorite.

Makes 1 pie

1. Make the dough and refrigerate it for at least an hour, or overnight. Roll out the bottom crust and place it in a 9- to 10-inch pie plate. Tuck the crust into the plate, trim the edges, and fold them into a ridge. Freeze the crust while you prepare the next steps of the recipe.

2. Preheat the oven to 425 degrees F.

3. To make the topping, in the bowl of a food processor, combine the flour, brown sugar, granulated sugar, cinnamon, and salt. Pulse until combined. Add the pecans and pulse just to combine. Scatter butter chunks over the surface of the dry ingredients. Process with 10 one-second pulses. The mixture should resemble bread crumbs. If it doesn't, pulse a few times more. Refrigerate the topping while you make the filling.

4. To make the filling, in a large bowl, mix the apples with the brown sugar, whiskey, cinnamon, nutmeg, and salt. Taste and adjust the flavors as needed. Stir in the flour and butter.

5. Retrieve the crust from the freezer.

continued

½ recipe any double-crust pie dough (for a single crust)

For the crumble topping:

¾ cup flour

¼ cup (packed) light brown sugar

¼ cup granulated sugar

½ teaspoon ground cinnamon

½ teaspoon salt

½ cup chopped pecans

6 tablespoons chilled unsalted butter, cut into large chunks

For the filling:

5 or 6 (about 2 pounds) tart pie apples, peeled if desired, cored, and thinly sliced

½ cup (packed) light brown sugar

2 to 3 tablespoons whiskey or bourbon (add the extra shot if you'd like a boozier pie)

½ teaspoon ground cinnamon

¼ teaspoon ground nutmeg

Pinch of salt

2 tablespoons flour

2 tablespoons chilled unsalted butter, cut into small pieces

6. Mound the apples into the bottom crust and press them down gently to eliminate air holes. Retrieve the topping from the fridge and sprinkle it evenly over the top.

7. Bake the pie in the middle of the oven for 15 minutes, or until the bottom crust looks dry, blistered, and blond. Reduce the heat to 350 degrees F for 40 to 50 minutes more, until the crumble browns, the juices bubble slow and thick at the pie's edge, and the apples yield easily when pierced by a sharp knife.

8. Cool on a wire rack for at least a few hours before serving. Serve warm or at room temperature. Store leftovers on the kitchen counter loosely wrapped in a towel for up to 3 days.

❧ GINGER-HONEY APPLE PIE ❧

I'd argue that this is the coziest pie in the whole chapter. Like a sweet version of chicken noodle soup, it warms an autumn kitchen and cures the postsummer blues. This pie, too, was adapted by *Bubby's Homemade Pies.*

Makes 1 pie

1. Make the dough and refrigerate it for at least an hour, or overnight. Roll out the bottom crust and place it in a 9- to 10-inch pie plate. Tuck the crust into the plate and trim the edges. Refrigerate the crust while you prepare the next steps of the recipe.

2. Preheat the oven to 425 degrees F.

3. In a small saucepan over medium-low heat, warm the honey and ginger until the honey is liquid. Put the apples in a large bowl and add the lemon juice, cayenne, and salt. Pour the honey in and stir gently to combine. Taste and adjust the flavors as needed. Stir in the flour and set the filling aside.

4. Roll out the top crust and retrieve the bottom crust from the refrigerator.

continued

1 recipe any double-crust pie dough

¾ cup clover honey

2 tablespoons peeled, finely chopped fresh ginger

5 or 6 (about 2 pounds) tart pie apples, peeled if desired, cored, and thinly sliced

Juice of 1 medium lemon (2 to 3 tablespoons)

Pinch of cayenne

Pinch of salt

3 tablespoons flour

2 tablespoons chilled unsalted butter, cut into small pieces

Egg white wash (1 egg white beaten with 1 teaspoon water)

Demerara sugar, for sprinkling

5. Using a slotted spoon, put the apples in the bottom crust, pressing them down gently to pack them into the pie. Pour in the liquid from the filling, stopping about a ½ inch below the rim. Discard any leftover liquid. Smooth the filling into a mound with your hands and dot it with the butter. Drape the top crust over it, trim the edges, and crimp or flute them. Cut generous steam vents, brush the crust with the egg white wash, and sprinkle it with the demerara sugar.

6. Bake the pie in the middle of the oven for 15 to 20 minutes, until the crust is blond and blistered. Rotate the pie front to back and reduce the heat to 375 degrees F. Bake for 35 to 45 minutes more, until the crust is deeply golden and the juices bubble slowly at the pie's edge.

7. Cool on a wire rack for at least an hour. Serve warm or at room temperature. Store leftovers on the kitchen counter loosely wrapped in a towel for up to 3 days.

❖ THREE PEAR AND GOUDA PIE ❖

Choose at least three varieties of almost-ripe pears to create an ultra-peary, velvet-textured filling. Aged or smoked Gouda are more assertive than softer, younger Goudas, though all types of this creamy cheese make delicious cheesy pastry. This pie is all about the pear/Gouda combination, a warm contrast of flavors that lets this pie straddle the fence between savory and sweet.

Makes 1 pie

1. Make the dough and refrigerate it for at least an hour, or overnight. Roll out the bottom crust and place it in a 9- to 10-inch pie plate. Tuck the crust into the plate and trim the edges. Refrigerate the crust while you prepare the next steps of the recipe.

2. Preheat the oven to 425 degrees F.

3. Core and slice the pears very thinly—⅛ inch, if possible. In a medium bowl, mix the pears with the sugar, lemon juice, nutmeg, and salt. Taste and adjust the flavors as needed. Gently stir in the flour and set the filling aside.

4. Roll out the top crust and retrieve the bottom crust from the refrigerator.

5. Pile the pears into the bottom crust and gently pack them down to eliminate air holes. Smooth the pears into a mound with your hands and dot them with the butter. Drape the top crust over the filling. Trim, fold, and flute the edges if you like. Cut generous steam vents, brush the crust with the egg white wash, and sprinkle it with the salt.

continued

1 recipe Cheese Crust (page 68), with hard aged Gouda or smoked Gouda

2 ripe Bartlett pears

2 ripe D'Anjou pears

2 ripe Bosc pears

¼ cup sugar

Juice of ½ medium lemon (about 1½ tablespoons)

Pinch of ground nutmeg

Pinch of salt

3 tablespoons flour

2 tablespoons chilled unsalted butter, cut into small pieces

Egg white wash (1 egg white beaten with 1 teaspoon water)

Coarse salt

6. Bake the pie in the middle of the oven for 15 to 20 minutes, until the crust is blond and blistered. Rotate the pie front to back and reduce the heat to 375 degrees F. Bake for 35 to 45 minutes more, until the crust is deeply golden and the juices bubble slowly at the pie's edge.

7. Cool the pie on a wire rack for at least an hour before serving. Serve warm or at room temperature. Store leftovers on the kitchen counter loosely wrapped in a towel for up to 3 days.

❖ APPLE PEAR CRANBERRY PIE ❖

This is my Christmas special, with bright baubles of bitter-tart cranberries in an otherwise sweet green apple-pear filling.

Makes 1 pie

1. Make the dough and refrigerate it for at least an hour, or overnight. Roll out the bottom crust and place it in a 9- to 10-inch pie plate. Tuck the crust into the plate and trim the edges. Refrigerate the crust while you prepare the next steps of the recipe.

2. Preheat the oven to 425 degrees F.

3. Put the apple and pear slices in a large bowl and squeeze the lemon juice over them to prevent browning. Stir in the cranberries, granulated sugar, candied ginger, cinnamon, nutmeg, and salt. Taste and adjust the flavors as needed. Gently stir in the flour and set the filling aside.

4. Roll out the top crust and retrieve the bottom crust from the refrigerator.

5. Pile the filling into the bottom crust and gently pack the fruit down to eliminate air holes. Mound it with your hands, and dot it with the butter. Drape the top crust over it and trim, fold, and flute the edges if you like. Cut generous steam vents, brush the crust with the egg white wash, and sprinkle it with the demerara sugar.

continued

1 recipe any double-crust pie dough

2 Gravenstein or Granny Smith apples, peeled if desired, cored, and thinly sliced

2 any variety ripe pears, cored and thinly sliced

Juice of ½ medium lemon (about 1½ tablespoons)

1 cup fresh or frozen cranberries

1 cup granulated sugar

1 tablespoon finely chopped candied ginger

½ teaspoon ground cinnamon

¼ teaspoon ground nutmeg

Big pinch of salt

3 tablespoons flour

2 tablespoons chilled unsalted butter, cut into small pieces

Egg white wash (1 egg white beaten with 1 teaspoon water)

Demerara sugar, for sprinkling

6. Bake the pie in the middle of the oven for 15 to 20 minutes, until the crust is blond and blistered. Rotate the pie front to back and reduce the heat to 375 degrees F. Bake for 35 to 45 minutes more, until the crust is deeply golden and the juices bubble slowly at the pie's edge.

7. Cool the pie on a wire rack for at least an hour before serving. Serve warm or at room temperature. Store leftovers on the kitchen counter loosely wrapped in a towel for up to 3 days.

❧ APPLE, PORK SAUSAGE, AND ROSEMARY PIE ❧

This pie, on the sweet side of savory, was inspired by a plate of particularly good grilled kielbasa served with sautéed tart apples and spaetzle on the side. You can use chicken, pork, or lamb sausage, but this recipe was tested with a pork sausage that was very light on grease. If your sausage produces a significant amount of fat while browning, pour most of it off or use it to coat and thicken the apples instead of the unsalted butter called for here.

Makes 1 pie

1. Make the dough and refrigerate it for at least an hour, or overnight. Roll out the bottom crust and place it in a 9- to 10-inch pie plate. Tuck the crust into the plate and trim the edges. Refrigerate the crust while you prepare the next steps of the recipe.

2. Preheat the oven to 425 degrees F.

3. In a medium skillet over medium-high heat, brown the sausage, breaking it up with a spatula and stirring only occasionally until it is cooked through. Remove the pan from the heat, pour off any excess fat, and put the sausage in a large bowl. Stir in the apples, sugar, rosemary, salt, and flour. Set the filling aside and allow it to cool before rolling out the top crust—20 minutes in the refrigerator will do the trick.

4. Roll out the top crust and retrieve the bottom crust from the refrigerator.

continued

1 recipe any double-crust pie dough (omit the sugar)

¾ pound chicken or pork sausage (not Italian), bulk or removed from casings

4 tart pie apples, cored and cut in ½-inch dice (about 4 cups)

¼ cup sugar

1 teaspoon chopped rosemary

Pinch of salt

3 tablespoons flour

2 tablespoons chilled unsalted butter, cut into pieces

Egg white wash (1 egg white beaten with 1 teaspoon water)

Coarse salt

5. Pile the filling into the bottom crust, pressing down gently to pack it into the pie, and dot it with the butter. Drape the top crust over it and trim, fold, and flute the edges if you like. Cut generous steam vents, brush the crust with the egg white wash, and sprinkle it with the salt.

6. Bake the pie in the middle of the oven for 15 to 20 minutes, until the crust is blond and blistered. Rotate the pie front to back and reduce the heat to 375 degrees F. Bake for 35 to 45 minutes more, until the crust is deeply golden and the juices bubble slowly at the pie's edge.

7. Cool on a wire rack for half an hour and serve warm. Store leftovers tightly wrapped in the refrigerator.

❖ CRAB/APPLE PIE ❖

Crab apples are relatives of apples and pears, but in this pie they take after a different cousin—the rose. Ever notice that crab apples, which grow (often barely tended) wherever autumn is crisp and cool, look a lot like rose hips? That's no coincidence. Like quince (another relative), a raw crab apple is barely palatable, while a cooked one smells and tastes slightly of flowers. They're walnut-size but have an apple's core, so they require a patient knife to deseed and slice enough of them to make a pie. That's why this recipe only requires a cup. Their rosy flavor and rind turn an apple pie from dependable to dazzling.

Makes 1 pie

1. Make the dough and refrigerate it for at least an hour, or overnight. Roll out the bottom crust and place it in a 9- to 10-inch pie plate. Tuck the crust into the plate and trim the edges. Refrigerate it while you prepare the next steps of the recipe.

2. Preheat the oven to 425 degrees F.

3. Slice off the tops and bottoms of the crab apples and core them. They're tiny, so be careful not to cut too much of their edible fruit away. Slice the fruit as thinly as possible, leaving the rosy peel on. In a medium bowl, combine the crab apple slices with the granulated sugar and let them sit while you prepare the rest of the fruit.

4. Core, but don't peel (unless you want to) the apples and pear, and slice them as thinly as possible, no thicker than ¼ inch. Put the slices in a large bowl and squeeze the lemon juice over them to prevent browning. Add the crab apple-sugar mixture. Stir in the cinnamon, nutmeg, and salt. Taste and adjust the flavors as needed. Stir in the flour and set the filling aside.

continued

1 recipe any double-crust pie dough

2 or 3 big handfuls crab apples (for 1 cup sliced)

¾ cup granulated sugar, divided

3 or 4 tart pie apples (such as Gravenstein, Belle de Boskoop, Macoun, or Cortland)

1 any variety ripe pear

Juice of ½ medium lemon, or more (1 to 2 tablespoons)

½ teaspoon ground cinnamon

¼ teaspoon ground nutmeg

Big pinch of salt

3 tablespoons flour

2 tablespoons chilled unsalted butter, cut into small pieces

Egg white wash (1 egg white beaten with 1 teaspoon water)

Demerara sugar, for sprinkling

5. Roll out the top crust and retrieve the bottom crust from the refrigerator.

6. Pile the sliced fruit in the bottom crust, pressing them down gently to pack them into the pie. If any liquid remains in the bowl, pour it over the fruit. Smooth the filling into a mound with your hands and dot it with the butter. Drape the top crust over it, trim the edges, and crimp or flute them. Cut generous steam vents, brush the crust with the egg white wash, and sprinkle it with the demerara sugar.

7. Bake the pie in the middle of the oven for 15 to 20 minutes until the crust is blond and blistered. Rotate the pie front to back and reduce the heat to 375 degrees F. Bake for 35 to 45 minutes more, until the crust is deeply golden and the juices bubble slowly at the pie's edge.

8. Cool the pie on a wire rack for at least an hour before serving. Serve warm or at room temperature. Store leftovers on the kitchen counter loosely wrapped in a towel for up to 3 days.

❖ ROSE FAMILY PIE ❖

Apples, pears, and quince (all members of the Rosaceae, or rose, family) cozy up with honey and cinnamon for a pie that, in my family, eclipses all other Thanksgiving pies.

Quinces take longer to bake than their softer cousins. Sautéing them in butter helps them get a head start. Choose a light, floral honey to frame the fruit. Their natural pectin requires only a spoonful of thickening flour. The ¼ cup of butter in this recipe is as much for rich flavor as it is for thickening power.

Makes 1 pie

1. Make the dough and refrigerate it for at least an hour, or overnight. Roll out the bottom crust and place it in a 9- to 10-inch pie plate. Tuck the crust into the plate and trim the edges. Refrigerate the crust while you prepare the next steps of the recipe.

2. Preheat the oven to 425 degrees F.

3. In a large skillet over medium heat, melt the butter. Add the quince slices, stir to coat, and sauté until tender, stirring occasionally to prevent browning. Quince cook quite slowly and can be sour if undercooked, so be patient and make sure they're soft before you remove them from the heat.

4. In a medium bowl, combine the quince, pears, apples, honey, cinnamon, nutmeg, and salt, and stir until each slice is evenly covered. Taste and adjust the flavors as needed. Stir in the flour and set the filling aside.

continued

1 recipe any double-crust pie dough

¼ cup (½ stick) unsalted butter

2 quinces (about 1 pound) peeled, cored, and sliced ⅛ inch thick

2 pears, any variety, peeled if desired, cored, and sliced ⅛ inch thick

2 tart pie apples, peeled if desired, cored, and sliced ⅛ inch thick

½ cup honey

½ teaspoon ground cinnamon

Small pinch of ground nutmeg

Pinch of salt

1 heaping tablespoon flour

Egg white wash (1 egg white beaten with 1 teaspoon water)

Demerara sugar, for sprinkling

Quince is apple's complicated older cousin. Some might call her old-fashioned—early references to apples (for example, in the Bible) were probably actually talking about quince. Raw quince smells heavenly—like roses and honey—but tastes astringent and mouth-puckeringly dry. Quince must be cooked to become palatable.

Though it was fashionable to plant a quince tree in the corner of the orchard during colonial times, quince has steadily lost ground to fruit with more mass-market appeal. You can find them now at fancy grocery stores, food co-ops, and farmers' markets. My supply comes from a friend's farm south of Portland, Oregon. They arrive around Halloween and have incredible staying power. Stored in the refrigerator, a sack of them was perfectly edible three months later.

5. Roll out the top crust and retrieve the bottom crust from the refrigerator.

6. Pour the filling into the bottom crust and mound it with your hands. Drape the top crust over it. Trim, fold, and flute the edges if you like. Cut generous steam vents, brush the crust with the egg white wash, and sprinkle it with the demerara sugar.

7. Bake the pie in the middle of the oven for 15 to 20 minutes, until the crust is blond and blistered. Rotate the pie front to back and reduce the heat to 375 degrees F. Bake for 35 to 45 minutes more, until the crust is deeply golden and the juices bubble slowly at the pie's edge. If the crust starts to get too brown, tent it with aluminum foil.

8. Cool the pie on a wire rack for at least an hour before serving. Serve warm or at room temperature. Store leftovers on the kitchen counter loosely wrapped in a towel for up to 3 days.

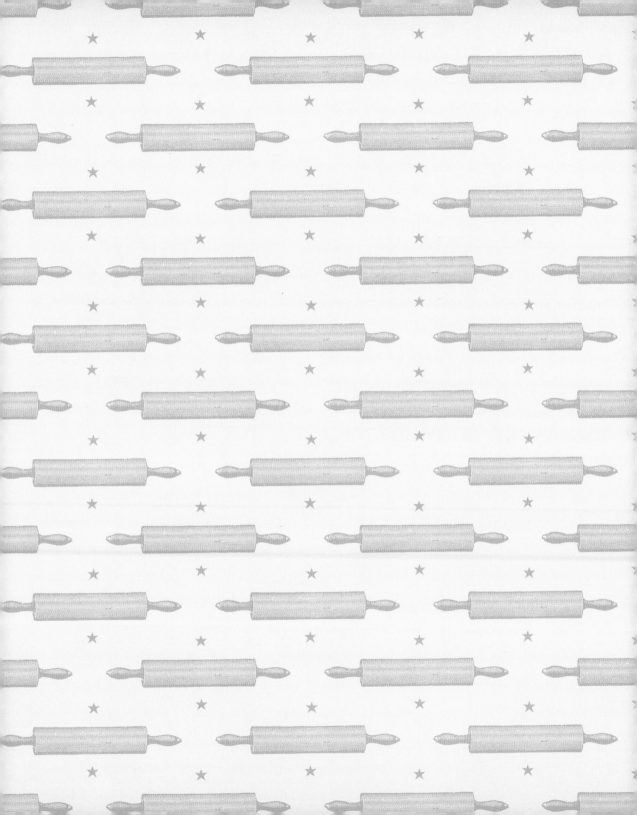

snow cupboard pies

. . . such a spring is brief; / by five o'clock
the chill of sundown, / darkness, the blue TVs
flashing like storms / in the picture windows . . .

—"LATE FEBRUARY," TED KOOSER

★　★　★　★　★

Fruit is time.

To paraphrase Li-Young Lee's poem "From Blossoms," fruit is the water, the sun, the dust, and the days. Pie made with fruit is season-bound, part of an entire year's arc. While I celebrate what's in season by putting it in a pie, I'm anxious to get my share of the harvest, to use it before it rots, all while anticipating the next crop. I could say I miss the pies I can't make until next year, but that's not quite right. Time is passing, that's all. Every day lived is a necessary loss that we each, in our own way, strive to accept or deny, or simply make sweeter. The joy I take in making and eating fruit pie is inextricable from the sense that the season's riches were well spent, but spent nonetheless. Until next year.

At no time is this more evident than winter. That's when we go without. When the warmer months return to us in the disguise of stored food. There's mention of something called a "snow cupboard" in *Farm Journal's Complete Pie Cookbook*, and I like that idea—a cache of food stored up in case of bad weather. During the out-of-season season, we pull from our snow cupboards to make pies out of canned, dried, or otherwise preserved goodies. I lump hot-weather fruits into my snow cupboard too, only because lemons and coconuts and bananas never grow in my cool home state, so for me they're always out of season.

The recipes that follow are made with shelf-stable ingredients that remain high quality despite being preserved, or with fresh fruit from warm states that's in season during the cold months, when we need their culinary sunshine to keep us sane until spring.

❧ BANANA CREAM PIE ❧

I know, I know. In the introduction I said there would be no cream pies. I was wrong! I contain multitudes! For this particular banana cream pie, I'll make an exception.

My acquaintance with this pie came while I was sitting on the counter of Chicago's Bang Bang pie shop. Megan Miller, Bang Bang's co-owner and head baker, set it beside me shortly after I finished reading "Banana Cream," a poem from my book *A Commonplace Book of Pie*. I watched her dip a pie server in hot water before every slice, ensuring a clean cut so the pie slices stood up neatly on the plate instead of smooshing into a pudding puddle like most versions of banana cream. She sprinkled each slice with brown sugar and served them with tiny forks she and her husband had foraged from antique stores. Their short tines made each sweet bite no bigger than a taste.

Makes 1 pie

1. Make the dough and refrigerate it for at least an hour, or overnight. Roll out the bottom crust and place it in a 9- to 10-inch pie plate. Tuck the crust into the plate, trim the edges, and tuck the edges into the rim of the plate. Flute or crimp the edges if you want to.

2. Blind bake the crust according to the instructions in "How to Bake Blind" (page 49), and cool on a wire rack for at least an hour before filling.

3. Using a wooden spoon, mix the egg yolks and cornstarch in a small bowl. Set the mixture aside. In a large heavy-bottomed pot, combine the milk, 1 cup of the cream, ½ cup of the granulated sugar, and the salt. Over low heat, warm the mixture until it's hot to the touch but not boiling.

continued

½ recipe Extra-Flaky Piecrust (page 61)

4 egg yolks

⅓ cup cornstarch

2 cups whole milk

1½ cups heavy cream, divided

½ cup plus 1 teaspoon granulated sugar, divided

¼ teaspoon salt

2 tablespoons butter

2 teaspoons vanilla extract

Pinch of ground nutmeg

3 to 4 ripe bananas

Brown sugar, for sprinkling

4. Stir a tablespoon of the hot cream mixture into the egg mixture until combined, then another and another, whisking the whole time, until you've used up all the cream. The egg mixture should be liquid and easy to pour. Pour it back into the pot and increase the heat to medium-high.

5. Cook the custard, stirring constantly and scraping the bottom of the pot, until it is thick and boiling, about 5 to 10 minutes. Reduce the heat to medium-low and let the custard simmer for 6 minutes, stirring constantly. Remove the pan from the heat, stir in the butter and vanilla, and let the mixture cool, stirring occasionally to prevent lumps.

6. Once the custard is lukewarm and thickened, use an electric hand mixer to beat in ¼ cup of the cream. Beat for as long as it takes to bring the custard to your desired thickness—for me, that's the moment when the beaters leave a pile of creamy ruffles that hold their shape long after the beater passes through. Pour the custard into the piecrust and sprinkle the nutmeg over the top. Refrigerate the pie for an hour, or until it is firmly set. Just before you're ready to serve the pie, thinly slice the bananas and arrange them on the top of the pie.

7. In a medium chilled metal bowl, beat the remaining ¼ cup cream with the remaining 1 teaspoon sugar until stiff. Spread it over the bananas, sprinkle each slice with the brown sugar, and serve immediately.

8. Store leftovers in the refrigerator. Wrap them in plastic or cover the pie with a large bowl to prevent the custard from drying out.

❖ SHAKER LEMON PIE ❖

Shakers have a motto—"Hands to work and hearts to God"—that expresses how we can find meaning through hard work and worship. Simple design and painstaking craftsmanship are physical expressions of their devotion to God, the key characteristics of their famous furniture and their cuisine, including this Shaker Lemon Pie. Just two lemons, two cups of sugar, four eggs, a little salt, and a crust is all it takes to make this intensely sweet and tart pie. Meyer lemons work best here, the thinner-skinned, the better. In fact, don't bother with thick-skinned lemons at all, as they'll be too pithy. Start this pie the night before you want to bake it. To achieve intense sweetness and avoid too-tartness, the lemons must sit in sugar overnight.

Makes 1 pie

1. Wash the lemons and slice them in half lengthwise, keeping the peel on. Rest the flat surface on a cutting board and cut the lemon as paper-thin as you can into half-moon slices. Remove seeds as you go. Some people use a mandoline for this job; I like my fingertips too much, so I use a super-sharp chef's knife.

2. Put the lemon slices in a medium bowl, pour the granulated sugar over them, and let them sit overnight. This is important. If you use the lemons too soon, they won't be nearly sweet enough. After the first hour, stir them once. After that, give them a quick stir whenever you pass through the kitchen.

3. Preheat the oven to 425 degrees F. Roll out the bottom crust, place it in the pie pan, and refrigerate it while you mix the filling.

continued

2 large lemons

2 cups granulated sugar, plus more for sprinkling

1 recipe any double-crust pie dough

4 large eggs

Pinch of salt

Egg white wash (1 egg white beaten with 1 teaspoon water)

Demerara sugar, for sprinkling

A little secret for summer, should you choose to make this then: this is the only pie I'd ever suggest freezing after it's been baked. The freezer ruins the crust, sure, but creates an entirely different dessert—something like frozen lemonade in pillow-soft pastry.

4. In a small bowl, thoroughly beat the eggs. Add them, along with the salt, to the lemons and mix gently until combined.

5. Roll out the top crust and retrieve the bottom crust from the refrigerator.

6. Pour the filling into the bottom crust and drape the top crust over it. Trim the edges, and crimp or flute them. Cut generous steam vents. The top crust will wobble a bit, like a duvet on a waterbed. Some of the lemon filling may peek through the vents. That's just fine. Brush the crust with the egg white wash and sprinkle it with the demerara sugar.

7. Bake for 15 minutes, then reduce the heat to 375 degrees F and bake for 30 to 35 minutes more, until the top crust is golden brown. About halfway through, rotate the pie front to back to ensure even baking. Cool on a wire rack and serve warm or at room temperature.

8. Store leftovers on the kitchen counter loosely wrapped in a towel for up to 3 days.

❖ COCONUT CHESS PIE ❖

True fans of chess pie and Southern cooking will probably laugh that I'm calling this a chess pie, which normally would be a simple preparation of eggs, butter, sugar, and maybe some vanilla or raisins. My version uses coconut milk and a heap of coconut flakes to make an over-the-top coconut pie that is more modest than a coconut cream, but just as rich. Call it a macaroon pie, maybe.

Makes 1 pie

1. Make the dough and refrigerate it for at least an hour, or overnight. Roll out the bottom crust and place it in a 9-inch pie plate. Tuck the crust into the plate, trim the edges, and fold them into a ridge. Freeze the crust while you prepare the next steps of the recipe.

2. Preheat the oven to 350 degrees F.

3. With an electric hand mixer, beat the eggs and sugar for about 2 minutes on medium speed until thoroughly mixed and a little frothy. Stir in the coconut milk, 1 cup of the flaked coconut, the butter, and salt. Pour the filling into the pie shell and bake for 1 hour. If the top starts getting too brown, cover it with aluminum foil. (It should look toasty on top, but not burned.) When the center of the pie is a little soft and the edges are firm, the pie is done.

4. Allow the pie to cool completely on a wire rack (at least a few hours) before serving. Sprinkle the toasted flaked coconut over the pie right before serving. Serve at room temperature or chilled.

5. Store leftovers in the refrigerator for up to 3 days.

½ recipe any double-crust pie dough (for a single crust)

3 eggs

1 cup sugar

1 cup coconut milk

1 cups (2 ounces) unsweetened flaked coconut

⅓ cup butter, melted

Big pinch of salt

½ cups (1 ounces) toasted unsweetened flaked coconut

To toast the flaked coconut, spread it on a cookie sheet and bake for 5 to 10 minutes at 325 degrees F. It will toast quickly, so keep an eye on it.

❖ WHISKEY MAPLE PECAN PIE ❖

Sugar, nuts, butter, and eggs—that's a pecan pie. This version passes up the usual Karo syrup in favor of more complex natural sugars, plus a slug of whiskey to add an extra buzz to sugar's high. This is, by far, the sweetest pie in the book.

Makes 1 pie

½ recipe any double-crust pie dough (for a single crust)

3 large eggs

¾ cup maple syrup

¾ cup (packed) light brown sugar

¼ cup (½ stick) unsalted butter, melted

1 teaspoon white vinegar

3 tablespoons rye whiskey

¼ teaspoon salt

2 cups pecan halves

1. Make the dough and refrigerate it for at least an hour, or overnight. Roll out the bottom crust and place it in a 9-inch pie plate. Tuck the crust into the plate, trim the edges, and fold them into a ridge. Freeze the crust while you prepare the next steps of the recipe.

2. Preheat the oven to 350 degrees F.

3. In a medium bowl, beat the eggs with an electric hand mixer until frothy. Stir in the maple syrup, brown sugar, butter, vinegar, whiskey, and salt. Mix in the pecans. Pour the filling into the pie shell and smooth the surface with a spoon. Bake for 50 to 55 minutes, until the crust is golden and the center remains firm when gently shaken.

4. Cool on a wire rack for at least an hour before serving. Serve warm or at room temperature.

5. Store leftovers on the kitchen counter loosely wrapped in a towel for up to 3 days.

❖ CHERRY CRANBERRY PIE ❖

The seasons of these fruits couldn't be more mismatched (cranberries in December, cherries in July), which means you'll end up using at least one kind of frozen fruit to make this recipe. But that also means, December or July, this sweet-and-sour pie is a sunbreak, perfect for breakfast or Christmas dessert.

Top with a lattice crust, if you like. Or turn this into a galette by using the Galette Dough (page 70), following all other instructions as is.

Makes 1 pie

1 recipe any double-crust pie dough

3 cups fresh or frozen pie cherries

2 cups fresh or frozen cranberries

1 cup granulated sugar

Juice of ½ medium lemon (about 1½ tablespoons)

1 teaspoon almond extract

Pinch of ground nutmeg

Pinch of salt

⅓ cup flour

2 tablespoons unsalted butter, cut into small pieces

Egg white wash (1 egg white beaten with 1 teaspoon water)

Demerara sugar, for sprinkling

1. Make the dough and refrigerate it for at least an hour, or overnight. Roll out the bottom crust and place it in a 9- to 10-inch pie plate. Tuck the crust into the plate and trim the edges. Refrigerate the crust while you prepare the next steps of the recipe.

2. Preheat the oven to 425 degrees F.

3. In a large bowl, combine the cherries and cranberries with the granulated sugar, lemon juice, almond extract, nutmeg, and salt. Taste and adjust the flavors as needed. Stir in the flour and butter and set the filling aside.

4. Roll out the top crust and cut into strips for a lattice (if you wish). Retrieve the bottom crust from the refrigerator.

5. Pour the filling into the bottom crust, mound it with your hands, and drape the top crust over it. Trim, fold, and flute the edges if you like (see "How to Weave a Classic Lattice," page 50). Cut generous steam vents (if you're not making a lattice), brush the crust with the egg white wash, and sprinkle it with the demerara sugar.

6. Bake the pie in the middle of the oven for 15 to 20 minutes, or until the crust looks dry, blistered, and blond. Reduce the heat to 375 degrees F. Bake for at least 35 to 45 minutes more, rotating the pie front to back about halfway through to ensure even baking, until the crust is deeply golden and the juices are thickened and bubble slowly through the vents.

7. Allow the pie to cool completely on a wire rack. Serve warm or at room temperature. Store leftovers on the kitchen counter loosely wrapped in a towel for up to 3 days.

chiffon pie chic

Strawberry Chiffon Pie
with Vanilla Crumb Crust   202

Raspberry Chiffon Pie
with Chocolate Cookie Crust   204

Lemon Chiffon Pie
with Gingersnap Crust   207

Black Cherry Chiffon Pie
with Chocolate Cookie Crust   209

Gluten-Free Pumpkin Chiffon Pie
with Almond Flour Crust   211

I have made a pact with Sylvia that when I don't want cream chiffon pies & all the other fairy palace dishes it's not because she isn't an exquisite cook but because she cooks for relaxation while I eat only by necessity.

—TED HUGHES ON SYLVIA PLATH'S BAKING
HABITS, LETTER TO HIS BROTHER, 1957

★　★　★　★　★

If making a chiffon pie feels like blowing up a bright balloon of sugar, fruit, and cream, then eating one feels like a bite of pure color, like what would happen if the pastel glow of an Easter egg was the most edible thing about it. Thanks to whipped egg whites, chiffon's texture is as fine and ethereal as a Gibson Girl's topknot. Thanks to gelatin, this delicacy keeps a steel grip on fresh fruit while standing straight and graceful on a plate. If old-fashioned femininity were a pie, this would be it, the ultimate twentieth-century hostess. No wonder it's named after a party dress.

"Chiffon" is Americanese for Bavarian cream, a custard much like pastry cream, but airy with egg whites and firm with gelatin. The filling is usually unbaked and poured into a baked pie shell. If the filling has an egg-yolk base, it's heated before the addition of fruit and egg whites. Bringing the mixture to just-before-boiling breaks down the protein in the egg yolk that would prevent the filling from setting as it cools.

The most useful talent of this retro delight is its ability to frame fresh fruit like strawberries and sweet cherries—fruit that would be overwhelmed by heat in a baked pie. Another talent: it ages well. I've kept leftovers for a week in the refrigerator and noticed only a slightly soggy crust. That means you can make this a day or two ahead of serving time. You can also freeze the fully chilled pie (to allow the gelatin time to set up first) for up to three weeks. Thaw it in the refrigerator before serving, or try serving it frozen.

Many original chiffon recipes ask readers to whip another ½ cup of cream and spread it over the top of the pie or serve it on the side. I found these pies, with the exception of pumpkin chiffon, already creamy and too rich for more whipped cream, so I left the extra out. Add it back in if you like.

A warning: raw egg lies ahead. When making and storing these pies, use common sense.

★ ★ ★ ★ ★

on meringue

The meringue you'll make for these pies is no different from that airy pouf of sugar you've encountered on lemon meringue pies. However, we won't bake our meringue. Instead, we'll fold it into fruit, sugar, cream, and gelatin to give chiffon pie fillings the light texture they're named for.

Meringue is egg white and sugar whipped into a stiff foam. The best way to make meringue is to separate cold eggs while making sure to let no part of the yolk remain with the whites, as the yolk's fat will interfere with the egg whites' whipability. Lift any errant yolk out of the whites with a piece of eggshell, not your hands, which will leave oil in the whites. Let the whites come to room temperature (this, too, helps them whip). Beat them on high with a hand mixer in a very clean metal bowl until they form soft peaks. Test them by lifting the beaters out of the whites. When peaks form and droop where the beaters were, they're "soft." Add the sugar specified by the recipe in a slow stream, beating on high, until the mixture makes stiff peaks. You can check this by lifting the beaters out of the mixture again. If the sweet whites form a peak that stays put, they deserve the name "meringue."

❧ STRAWBERRY CHIFFON PIE
with VANILLA CRUMB CRUST ❧

From its featherweight name to its bright-pink filling, strawberry chiffon pie trembles with cheerfulness. That's certainly how I felt after discovering this ingenious way to suspend raw, juicy strawberries in pie filling. The trembling might have been a sugar high, but the cheerfulness was all strawberry.

This is an adapted classic from the 1965 edition of *The Farm Journal's Complete Pie Cookbook*. They suggest a graham cracker crust, but I prefer a vanilla crumb crust.

Makes 1 pie

1 recipe Any-Cookie-Crumb Crust (page 76) made with vanilla wafers and baked according to instructions

2 cups (1 pint) fresh strawberries, trimmed and quartered

¾ cup sugar, divided

1 envelope unflavored gelatin

¼ cup cold water

½ cup hot water

4 teaspoons freshly squeezed lemon juice

⅛ teaspoon salt

½ cup chilled heavy cream

2 egg whites

Handful of perfectly ripe strawberries, sliced, for garnish

1. Prepare the vanilla crumb crust, bake it, and let it cool while you prepare the rest of the pie.

2. Chill a metal bowl and electric beaters in the freezer.

3. In a medium bowl, crush the strawberries. I like to do this with my hands, but a pastry cutter or fork will work just fine. Mix the berries with ½ cup of the sugar and let them sit for 30 minutes.

4. Pour the gelatin into a small bowl, pour the cold water over it, and stir (this softens the gelatin). Then stir it into the hot water until dissolved. Add the gelatin to the crushed berries, along with the lemon juice and salt. Refrigerate the mixture. Briefly stir the mixture every 5 minutes while chilling to catch it at just the right setting stage—the mixture will lump softly when you drop it from the spoon back into the bowl. This will take 20 to 30 minutes.

5. Beat the chilled cream on high in the chilled bowl until it forms stiff peaks. Fold the whipped cream into the strawberry mixture.

6. Whip the egg whites with an electric beater on high until they hold soft peaks, then gradually add the remaining ¼ cup sugar as you beat the whites into stiff, glossy peaks. Fold the meringue into the strawberry mixture.

7. Pour the filling into the crust and smooth it into a mound with a spatula or spoon. Chill until completely set, about 2 to 3 hours. Garnish with the sliced fresh strawberries.

8. Serve chilled. Store leftovers under a large bowl in the fridge to protect the pie from off flavors and dry spots. Or drape the pie in plastic wrap. The filling will start to leak strawberry juice after a couple of days, which makes the crust soggy, so it's best to eat this within 2 days of making it.

Note that you'll need to stir the gelatin every 5 minutes while it is chilling to catch it at the right stage. If it sets too hard (when it begins to jiggle like Jell-O), you won't be able to smoothly incorporate the cream or meringue. If the gelatin over-sets, all is not lost. Gently heat the strawberry and gelatin mixture in a saucepan and stir until the mixture is liquid and smooth, then chill it again.

on strawberries

When it comes to baking, strawberries are a bit like apples. Those that taste best out of hand have a higher water and sugar content (I think "juicy" is the operative term here) and, when baked, turn into fruit soup. Unlike an apple (which, technically speaking, becomes mush instead of soup), a strawberry's sweetness dulls and cloys after a good stern cooking. It's sad, really. To wait all year for bright berries, only to wrap them in dough and destroy them with good intentions. If you're going to bake or make jam with strawberries, choose dry and firm Albions.

❧ RASPBERRY CHIFFON PIE
with CHOCOLATE COOKIE CRUST ❧

If you look closely, you'll notice this recipe is almost identical to Strawberry Chiffon Pie with Vanilla Crumb Crust (page 202)—the difference being the fruit and crust. Take that as an invitation to use this recipe as a changeable palette that will suit just about any berry.

═══ *Makes 1 pie* ═══

1 recipe Any-Cookie-Crumb Crust (page 76) made with chocolate cookies, baked and cooled

1½ pounds fresh raspberries, divided

¾ cup sugar, divided

1 envelope unflavored gelatin

¼ cup cold water

¼ cup hot water

Juice of ½ medium lemon (about 1 tablespoon)

⅛ teaspoon salt

½ cup chilled heavy cream

2 egg whites

1. Prepare the chocolate cookie crust, bake it, and let it cool while you prepare the rest of the pie.

2. Chill a metal bowl and electric beaters in the freezer.

3. In a medium bowl, smash half of the raspberries. I like to do this with my hands, but a pastry cutter or fork will work just fine. Mix the berries with ½ cup of the sugar and let them sit for 30 minutes.

4. Pour the gelatin into a small bowl, pour the cold water over it, and stir (this softens the gelatin). Then stir it into the hot water until dissolved. Add it to the smashed berries, along with the lemon juice and salt. Refrigerate the mixture, stirring every 5 minutes, until it starts to mound when dropped from a spoon, about 20 to 30 minutes.

5. With an electric beater, whip the chilled cream in the chilled bowl on high until it forms stiff peaks. Fold the whipped cream into the raspberry mixture.

6. Beat the egg whites with an electric mixer on high until they form soft peaks, then gradually add the remaining ¼ cup sugar as you beat the whites into stiff, glossy peaks. Fold the meringue into the raspberry mixture, along with a quarter of the remaining raspberries.

7. Pour the filling into the crust and smooth it into a mound with a spoon. Push the remaining raspberries gently into the filling so they sit like gumdrops on top of the pie. Chill until completely set, about 2 to 3 hours.

8. Serve chilled. Store leftovers under a large bowl in the fridge to protect the pie from off flavors and dry spots. Or drape the pie in plastic wrap. The pie will taste best when eaten within 3 days.

Note that you'll need to stir the gelatin every 5 minutes while it is chilling to catch it at the right stage. If it sets too hard (when it begins to jiggle like Jell-O), you won't be able to smoothly incorporate the cream or meringue. If the gelatin over-sets, all is not lost. Gently heat the raspberry and gelatin mixture in a saucepan and stir until the mixture is liquid and smooth, then chill it again.

❧ LEMON CHIFFON PIE
with GINGERSNAP CRUST ❧

Mid-century cookbooks call for all kinds of awkward preparations of chiffon. My least favorite of the midcentury versions I tried was an almond cream pie that asked me to boil a pot of water, then float a metal bowl in it, then beat a mixture of eggs, heavy cream, and gelatin with an electric beater while the bowl floated in the boiling water for exactly twelve minutes. I fully expected the next step to be "balance on one foot while singing 'The Star-Spangled Banner.'"

This preparation is not quite as simple as the easy mix and fold of the Strawberry Chiffon Pie with Vanilla Crumb Crust (page 202) and Raspberry Chiffon Pie with Chocolate Cookie Crust (page 204) recipes, but it's far simpler than electric beaters in floating bowls.

Lemon is always worth a little trouble. Lemon chiffon is like a lemon meringue pie whose layers have been folded together. *Farm Journal's Complete Pie Cookbook*, where I found the recipe I've adapted here, calls it "a refreshing dessert after a heavy meal."

=== *Makes 1 pie* ===

1. In a small, heavy-bottomed saucepan off the stove, combine the gelatin with ½ cup of the sugar and the salt. Mix well. In another bowl, beat the egg yolks with the water and lemon juice until combined. Stir the wet ingredients into the dry ingredients and cook over medium heat, stirring constantly, for about 5 minutes, or until the mixture barely comes to a boil.

2. Remove the pan from the heat and transfer the filling to a medium bowl. Stir in the lemon zest, and refrigerate the mixture until it has partially set, around 20 to 30 minutes. Briefly stir the mixture every 5 minutes while chilling to catch it at just the right setting stage—the mixture will lump softly when you drop it from the spoon back into the bowl.

continued

1 envelope unflavored gelatin

1 cup sugar, divided

⅛ teaspoon salt

4 eggs, separated

½ cup water

½ cup lemon juice (from about 3 medium lemons)

1 teaspoon lemon zest

1 recipe Any-Cookie-Crumb Crust (page 76) made with gingersnaps (unless they are bland, omit the cinnamon), baked and cooled

½ pint raspberries or blueberries, plus more for garnish (optional)

Note that you'll need to stir the gelatin every 5 minutes while it is chilling to catch it at the right stage. If it sets too hard (when it begins to jiggle like Jell-O), you won't be able to smoothly incorporate the cream or meringue. If the gelatin over-sets, all is not lost. Gently heat the lemon and gelatin mixture in a saucepan and stir until the mixture is liquid and smooth, then chill it again.

3. With an electric beater, whip the egg whites until soft peaks form. Gradually add the remaining ½ cup sugar and beat until the meringue is glossy and stiff. Fold the meringue into the filling, stirring gently from the bottom of the bowl until the filling's color is pale yellow with darker yellow flecks of zest.

4. Line the bottom of the crust with the berries. Pour in the filling until it almost threatens to flow over the crust. Refrigerate until completely set, about 2 to 3 hours. To garnish with more berries, check the filling in about 15 to 20 minutes. When the top is firm enough to hold the berries but still soft enough to easily nestle them into the filling, do that, arranging them in whatever sort of pattern looks nicest.

5. Serve chilled. Store leftovers under a large bowl in the fridge to protect the pie from off flavors and dry spots. Or drape the pie in plastic wrap. This pie keeps pretty well. After 3 days the crust might be a little soggy but the filling will still be dreamy.

❧ BLACK CHERRY CHIFFON PIE
with CHOCOLATE COOKIE CRUST ❧

My mother has fond memories of my father baking pie during their courting days, but her memories of the pie he made are not so sweet. She calls it a "Cherry Dream Pie" that got most of its cherry flavor from almond extract. What the dream part was made of she is no longer sure, but she thinks it may have been pure nostalgia—it was his mother's recipe. When I was writing this book, she asked me for a sweet cherry pie they could enjoy together. This is it.

Turns out chiffon is the long-awaited answer to the conundrum of how to use a sweet cherry in a cherry pie. Black cherries aren't just an invention of candy companies, they're a classification of cherry varieties, the other categories being sour (like Montmorency) red (like bing), and white (like Rainier). For this recipe I recommend dark-red, almost black Lapin cherries.

Makes 1 pie

1. Prepare the chocolate cookie crust, bake it, and let it cool while you prepare the rest of the pie.

2. Chill a metal bowl and electric beaters in the freezer.

3. In a small bowl, crush half of the cherries. I like to do this with my hands, but a pastry cutter or fork will work just fine. Using a sharp knife, cut half of the remaining cherries into quarters, and halve the rest. Set the cherries aside.

4. Mix the crushed cherries with ½ cup of the sugar and the lemon juice, and let them sit for 30 minutes.

continued

1 recipe Any-Cookie-Crumb Crust (page 76) made with chocolate cookies, baked and cooled

1½ pounds pitted fresh black cherries, divided

¾ cup sugar, divided

1 tablespoon freshly squeezed lemon juice

1 envelope unflavored gelatin

¼ cup cold water

¼ cup hot water

½ teaspoon almond extract

⅛ teaspoon salt

½ cup chilled heavy cream

2 egg whites

Make the crust in a 9- to 10-inch pie pan. There will be quite a lot of filling, so choose a deeper pan, if possible.

5. Pour the gelatin into a small bowl, pour the cold water over it, and stir (this softens the gelatin). Then stir it into the hot water until dissolved. Add it to the crushed cherries, along with the almond extract and salt. Refrigerate the mixture, stirring every 5 minutes, until it starts to mound when dropped from a spoon, about 20 to 30 minutes.

6. Whip the chilled cream in the chilled bowl with an electric beater on high until it forms stiff peaks. Once the filling has set, remove it from the refrigerator and fold in the whipped cream.

7. Beat the egg whites with an electric beater on high to soft peaks, then slowly add the remaining ¼ cup sugar as you beat the whites into stiff, glossy peaks. Fold the meringue into the filling, along with the quartered cherries.

8. Pour the filling into the crust and smooth it into a mound with the back of a wooden spoon. Push the halved cherries gently into the filling so they sit like gumdrops on top of the pie. Chill until completely set, about 2 to 3 hours.

9. Serve chilled. Store leftovers under a large bowl in the fridge to protect the pie from off flavors and dry spots. Or drape the pie in plastic wrap. This pie will taste best if eaten within 3 days.

Note that you'll need to stir the gelatin every 5 minutes while it is chilling to catch it at the right stage. If it sets too hard (when it begins to jiggle like Jell-O), you won't be able to smoothly incorporate the cream or meringue. If the gelatin over-sets, all is not lost. Gently heat the strawberry and gelatin mixture in a saucepan and stir until the mixture is liquid and smooth, then chill it again.

❖ GLUTEN-FREE PUMPKIN CHIFFON PIE
with ALMOND FLOUR CRUST ❖

Some of us love pumpkin pie and tradition. Some of us don't. I'm a fan of tradition, but not of pumpkin pie, so this chiffon pie has become a delicious compromise. Pumpkin traditionalists, don't knock this until you try it. The flavor is the same—still that pungent mix of cinnamon, ginger, and nutmeg that makes pumpkin into pie, still the dollop of whipped cream, still the dark orange smear left on your empty plate. But the texture is all new—light and airy, a delight instead of a holiday obligation.

Makes 1 pie

1. Make the crust and let it cool while you prepare the rest of the pie.

2. Set aside. In a heavy-bottomed saucepan off the stove, combine the milk and egg yolks, then stir in the brown sugar, salt, nutmeg, ginger, cinnamon, and gelatin until evenly mixed. Set the pan over medium heat and cook gently, stirring constantly, until the sugar and gelatin dissolve and the mixture thickens slightly. Don't let it boil.

3. Remove the mixture from the heat and let it cool. Add the pumpkin puree and the booze (if using). Whisk until combined. Refrigerate the mixture, stirring every 5 minutes, until it thickens enough to form soft mounds. This may take 20 to 30 minutes.

4. With an electric hand mixer, beat the egg whites to soft peaks. Slowly add ¼ cup of the granulated sugar and continue to beat until the egg whites form stiff, glossy peaks. Fold the meringue into the filling and pour the filling into the cooled crust. Refrigerate until set, an hour or two.

continued

1 recipe Gluten-Free Almond Flour Piecrust (page 75), baked and cooled

½ cup milk

3 eggs, separated

½ cup (packed) dark brown sugar

½ teaspoon salt

¼ teaspoon ground nutmeg, plus more for sprinkling

¼ teaspoon ground ginger

½ teaspoon ground cinnamon, plus more for sprinkling

1 envelope unflavored gelatin

1 (14-ounce) can pumpkin puree

¼ cup brandy, dark rum, or bourbon (optional)

¼ cup plus 2 tablespoons granulated sugar, divided

1 cup heavy cream

1 teaspoon vanilla extract

This pie is also delicious with a bottom crust made of gingersnaps (page 76) or pastry (Extra-Flaky, page 61, or Purple-Ribbon, page 66).

5. Fifteen minutes before serving, chill a metal bowl and electric beaters in the freezer. Beat the cream on high with the remaining 2 tablespoons granulated sugar and the vanilla until it forms hard peaks. Spread over the top of the pie, sprinkle with a little nutmeg and cinnamon.

6. Serve chilled. Store leftovers under a large bowl in the fridge to protect the pie from off flavors and dry spots. Or drape the pie in plastic wrap. This pie will taste best if eaten within 3 days.

à la mode: american style

Leave it to Americans to translate à la mode—French for "with style"—into "topped with ice cream."

I'm not against à la mode. I'm against the habit of it—how it's assumed there will be vanilla ice cream. All too often à la mode actually translates into the practice of using ice cream to cover up a whole host of pie sins, as if we were pouring gravy on burned steak. The pie you made can stand on its own, and it should.

This opinion (and my insistence on keeping that damn stuff away from my pie, even once "my" pie is on others' plates) has gotten me into trouble with my family and my students. It's a particularly American kind of trouble. When someone tells us how to live our lives, we think "Who the hell are you to tell me what to do?" We dig in our heels. We assert our independence.

I get that. I support that.

But please, for my sanity and for the sake of the beautiful pie you just made, let's make a compromise. Put the ice cream on the *side* of the pie. Not on top. Never on top.

Same goes for whipped cream and crème fraîche. On the side, please. Since these two toppers are easy to whip up and far more delicious when made by hand, I've included recipes for them here. For ice cream, head directly to the grocery store. Remember that vanilla isn't the only flavor—try ginger, lemon, or some other variety that will create a refreshing contrast with whatever pie you've chosen to serve.

continued

❧ Crème Fraîche ❧

You can buy this decadent and cultured creamy topping at the grocery store, sure, but it's better and cheaper homemade. All you need is a lidded container. I prefer a glass canning jar with a screw-top lid.

Don't use raw milk for this recipe—unless you know the cow, bacteria can make that a dicey decision. Pasteurized cream, not ultra-pasteurized, works best. If all you can find is ultra-pasteurized, you may need to wait a bit longer for results, and they'll probably taste less fresh.

Makes about 1 cup

1 cup heavy cream

2 tablespoons buttermilk or yogurt

In a small bowl, mix the cream and buttermilk, pour it into a glass jar, screw on the lid, and let the mixture sit in a warmish spot for a day. About halfway through the day, shake it like a Polaroid picture. Within 24 hours the mixture should thicken. If it has separated, stir it up. If it isn't as thick as you'd like, let it sit longer. Refrigerate the crème fraîche and use within a week or so. Serve pieside.

❧ Whipped Cream ❧

As classic as ice cream and easier to make. You can play around with different extracts to flavor the pie, or make this sweet and plain. My recipe includes vanilla extract because that pairs with just about everything.

For best results, thoroughly freeze a metal bowl and electric beaters before whipping. An hour in the freezer is beyond reproach; fifteen minutes is fine.

Makes about 1 cup

1 cup chilled heavy cream

2 tablespoons sugar

1 teaspoon vanilla extract

Beat the cream on high until it forms soft peaks, then slowly add the sugar and vanilla, beating on high as you go until the cream is thick and forms stiff peaks. Be careful not to beat too long after that—you could accidentally make butter (this is an exaggeration—unless you really whip the hell out of the cream). Spread over the top of the pie or serve pieside.

the gift of pie

The spirit of a gift is kept alive by its constant donation.

**—THE GIFT: CREATIVITY AND THE ARTIST IN
THE MODERN WORLD, LEWIS HYDE**

By the time my aunt Peg passed away from complications of a stroke, my uncle Dennis had lost thirty pounds. At the funeral, his suit hung loose. At home, their kitchen was organized and clean, full of Peg's mysterious cooking gadgets. We puzzled over a red plastic ring until a Google search finally revealed its true identity: open chip-bag sealer. Dennis threaded the crackling top of a bag through its mouth and left it on the counter, half empty.

Peg had a gift for gift-giving. When I was twelve, she blew my mind by sending me a basket of apple-scented lotion for Christmas. The girly daughter of a tomboy, I had no idea there were such things that could make a lady smell like an orchard. As far as I was concerned, my aunt had sent a basket of magic spells.

Two weeks before her stroke, Peg gave me three more gifts. The first was advice. Said as only someone who's been married since 1967 can say it: "When you're ready, and only when you're ready, Match.com is a perfectly suitable place to find a husband." The second was a gentle scolding: "Kate! You need to write your recipes down. You could have a cookbook!" The third arrived a week after she and Dennis flew home: a card with fifty bucks and a note—"Use this to buy something fun." Like mascara.

It was my mother's idea to make Dennis an apple pie. That got a smile out of him. Let's make two, I thought. "Katie, you can make the dough," he said, "but Peg will make the filling."

From the freezer he pulled two bags of frozen apple pie filling, labeled in careful black marker from the previous fall. "We bought a box of Cortlands and had a whole assembly line set up. My job was to peel them. Peggy did the rest." He plunked the filling into a bowl to thaw while I assembled dough from ingredients she had bought only weeks before. I can't remember what we talked about—pie, probably—but I do know it was a peaceful break from condolences and questions about the future.

With apple pie, Peggy got it right again. Exactly what her sweetheart needed to jumpstart his appetite, gain a little weight, start healing. She gave me what I needed too: to feel useful. "Such meals . . . remind us we're alive," writes the poet Kevin Young. Peg couldn't have known how much her apples would give us a sign of her love and care, sugar and sass. But she knew her gifts. She knew how to enjoy what she had while she had it, how to store something for the future, how to give the rest away.

She knew that pie is just fruit and flour, butter and sugar, spice and salt. That simplicity would help her express deeper truths. Gifts don't just nourish and delight. They sustain us with gratitude. A child's lesson, really, how to give and receive, but something that takes many of us the practice of a lifetime to perfect. Something that can itself be, like pie-making, a practice.

The pie was still steaming when I cut each of us a big slice. We ate slowly, careful not to burn our tongues, hoping our team effort would help my uncle clean his plate. Then we wrapped half the pie loosely in a towel and left it on the counter. Tomorrow's breakfast. A start.

acknowledgments

★ ★ ★ ★ ★

Good writing needs help. I've had more than my fair share. Huge and heartfelt thank you's go to these remarkable people:

To Gary Luke. This book exists because you asked for it.

To my dearest conspirators and collaborators, in art and in life: Kristen Millares Young, Emily Kendal Frey, Jessica Lynn Bonin, Katherine Eulensen, Annie Pardo, Whitney Ricketts.

To my family, for eating all the pie, and for loving me.

To the Heatons and the Neumayers. I love you.

To those who gave me shelter while I wrote this book: Lake Merwin Campers' Hideaway, Centrum Writers Conference, Lindsey and Tim Gadbois, Heather Malcolm, Marie McCaffrey, Lily Nickerson, Kate Schwartz, Melanie Sheehan, Michael Wiegers, Kary Wayson, and Brian Young.

To everyone who contributed their advice, words, encouragement, belief. And ate the pie. Especially Sam Ligon. Chelsey Slattum, Jamey Braden, Will and Beth Unger, Jennifer Borges Foster, Elizabeth Colen (even though you hate pie), Piper Daniels, Erin Belieu, Adam Boles, and Jude Dubois Countryman, thank you.

To Dani Cone and High 5 Pie for giving Pie School its first home.

To Evan Kirkley for giving Pie School style.

To Sara Fisher for teaching me how to describe taste.

To Amanda Manitach for asking me to write the essay that let me write the cookbook.

HUGE thanks to my amazing, patient, smart, and sweet-toothed recipe testers. I couldn't have written this book without you:

Marijo Adams, Paula Allen, Arianna Barrans, Michaela Brangan, Lyall Bush, Jeff Corey, Pete Erickson, Andrew Feld, Josie Friedman, Emily Hilliard, Rachel Hilsen, Christine Johnson-Duell, Julia Lipscomb, Maya Sonenberg, and Maria Turner-Carney.

To my Pie School students.

To Molly Wizenberg for writing, "Food is never just food."

To all my recipe sources, named and unnameable.

To Rina Jordan and Jenn Elliott Blake. You made this book beautiful.

To Anna Goldstein, Michelle Hope Anderson, and all the people at Sasquatch Books. I'm so proud to work with you.

suggested reading

(BOOKS THAT INSPIRED THIS BOOK)

★ ★ ★ ★ ★

Tamar Adler, *An Everlasting Meal*

Ruth Berolzheimer (editor),
  *The Victory Binding of the
  American Woman's Cook
  Book: Wartime Edition*

Jen Bervin and Ron Silver,
  Bubby's Homemade Pies

Jean Anthelme Brillat-Savarin,
  The Physiology of Taste

Janet Clarkson, *Pie: A Global History*

Tamasin Day-Lewis, *Tarts with
  Tops on*

Robert Farrar Capon, *The Supper
  of the Lamb*

MFK Fisher, *The Art of Eating*

Ken Haedrich, *Pie*

Janie Hibler, *The Berry Bible*

Nell B. Nichols (editor), *Farm
  Journal's Complete Pie Cookbook*

Laura Shapiro, *Perfection Salad*

Nigel Slater, *Ripe*

Alice B. Toklas, *The Alice B. Toklas
  Cookbook*

Kevin Young (editor), *The Hungry
  Ear: Poems of Food and Drink*

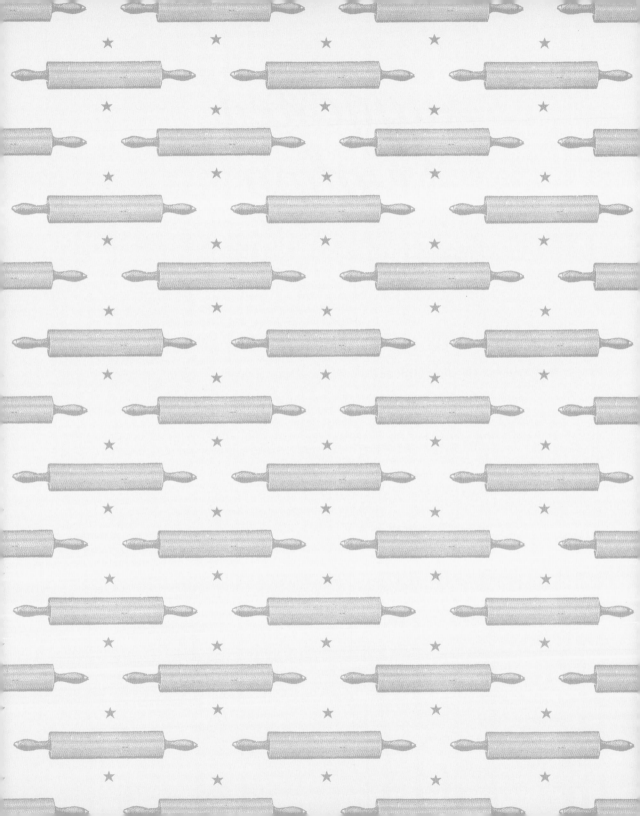

index

★ ★ ★ ★ ★

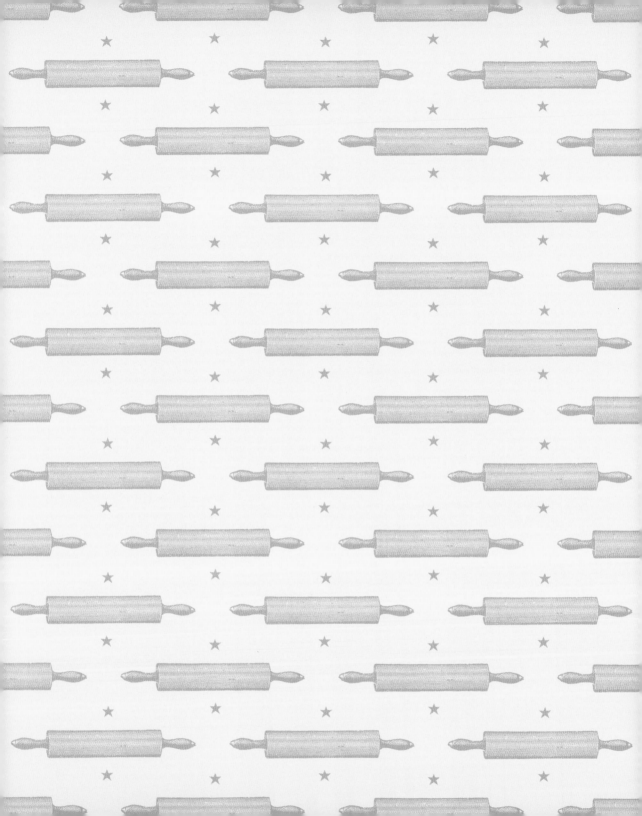

conversions

VOLUME

U.S.	METRIC	IMPERIAL
¼ tsp.	1.25 ml	
½ tsp.	2.5 ml	
1 tsp.	5 ml	
½ tbsp.	7.5 ml	
1 tbsp.	15 ml	
⅛ c.	30 ml	1 fl. oz.
¼ c.	60 ml	2 fl. oz.
⅓ c.	80 ml	2.5 fl. oz.
½ c.	125 ml	4 fl. oz.
1 c.	250 ml	8 fl. oz.
2 c. (1 pt.)	500 ml	16 fl. oz.
1 qt.	1 l	32 fl. oz.

LENGTH

U.S.	METRIC
⅛ in.	3 mm
¼ in.	6 mm
½ in.	1.25 cm
1 in.	2.5 cm
1 ft.	30 cm

WEIGHT

AVOIRDUPOIS	METRIC
¼ oz.	7 g
½ oz.	15 g
1 oz.	30 g
2 oz.	60 g
3 oz.	90 g
4 oz.	115 g
5 oz.	150 g
6 oz.	175 g
7 oz.	200 g
8 oz. (½ lb.)	225 g
9 oz.	250 g
10 oz.	300 g
11 oz.	325 g
12 oz.	350 g
13 oz.	375 g
14 oz.	400 g
15 oz.	425 g
16 oz. (1 lb.)	450 g
1½ lb.	750 g
2 lb.	900 g
2¼ lb.	1 kg
3 lb.	1.4 kg
4 lb.	1.8 kg

TEMPERATURE

OVEN MARK	FAHRENHEIT	CELSIUS	GAS
Very cool	250–275	130–140	½–1
Cool	300	150	2
Warm	325	165	3
Moderate	350	175	4
Moderately hot	375	190	5
	400	200	6
Hot	425	220	7
	450	230	8
Very Hot	475	245	9

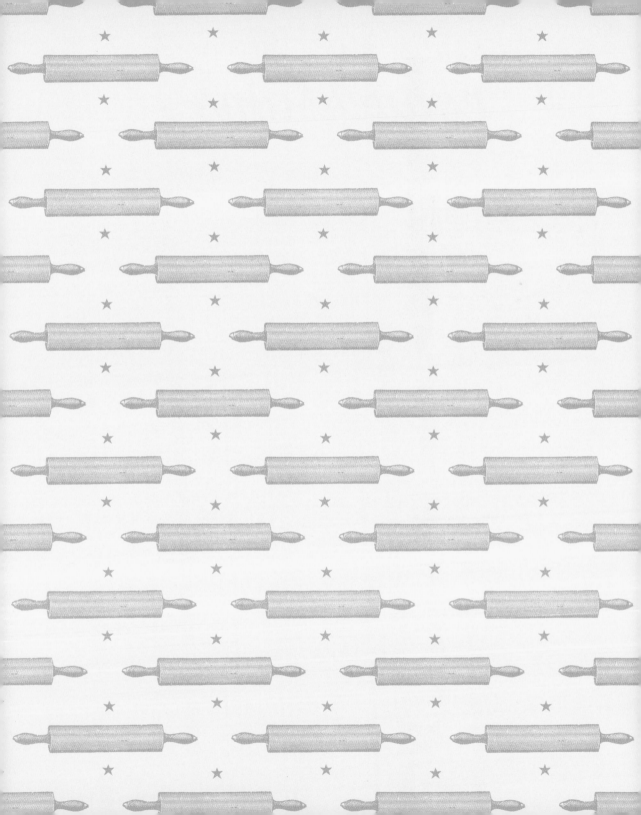

about the author

★ ★ ★ ★ ★

KATE LEBO is the author of *A Commonplace Book of Pie* (Chin Music Press, 2013) and *The Pie Lady's Manifesto*, a zine republished by *The Rumpus* in 2014. She founded Pie School, her roaming pastry academy, after graduating from the University of Washington's MFA program. Her poems have appeared in *Best New Poets*, *Gastronomica*, *Willow Springs*, and *AGNI*, among other journals, and she teaches creative writing workshops nationally. For more, visit KateLebo.com.